Whistling in the Dark

RICHARD MABEY

Whistling in the Dark

IN PURSUIT OF THE NIGHTINGALE

Aurum

Praise for
Whistling in the Dark

A book so delightful I must share it. It is poetry and
prose, natural history, memoir, myth and music . . .
and is full of the same darting rhythms as that
mysterious bird.
Simon Jenkins, *The Times*

A pure pleasure to read. It stimulates, nudges, tells
stories, argues and gleefully offends . . . I cannot
remember liking a book about nature as much as this
for years . . . It is a small classic.
Peter Levi, *Spectator*

What he accomplishes is exquisite and illuminating,
itself a sort of nightingale's song, variously throttling
back for a sub-theme, then ingeniously improvising
or swelling to full measure.
Euan Dunn, *The Countryman*

Quarto

This edition published in 2025 by Aurum,
an imprint of Quarto
One Triptych Place,
London, SE1 9SH
United Kingdom
www.Quarto.com/Aurum

EEA Representation, WTS Tax d.o.o., Žanova ulica 3, 4000 Kranj, Slovenia

First published in the United Kingdom in 1993 by Sinclair Stevenson,
an imprint of Random House.

A catalogue record for this book is available from the British Library.

ISBN: 978-1-83600-571-1
Ebook ISBN: 978-1-83600-572-8

10 9 8 7 6 5 4 3 2 1

Cover design by Paileen Currie
Typeset in Granjon LT Std by Typo•glyphix, Burton-on-Trent, DE14 3HE
Printed and bound by CPI Group (UK) Ltd, Croydon, CR0 4YY

For L.G., with love

Contents

Preface to
the new edition

It's become an annual ritual. Some time early in May, as close to the full moon as possible, we go to a common on the Suffolk coast to listen to the nightingales. It's a more poignant expedition each year. The birds always sing, but in smaller numbers, and in increasingly poor spring weather their songs can seem thinner and more hesitant. And to all of us who are aware of their declining numbers across Europe, they can sound like elegies. These yearly encounters have become a marker of time in both the birds' and our lives.

So it seemed an apt moment to issue a new edition of the book I wrote in the 1990s about the spell that the nightingale's songs have cast over humans for two millennia. It seems implausible, the way these piercing, unsettling arias – more than those of any other species of bird – have captivated listeners from Ovid and Provençal troubadours to Romantic poets and the very first bird song recordists. Is it just a consequence of a long-accumulated celebrity status? Or something intrinsic in the complex, oratorical performance that touches a deep chord in our understanding of what pure voice *is*, and can do?

These questions have risen again in the sense of loss the birds decline has prompted. Listeners nightwalk again, hold vigils, play music and sing in nightingale-haunted woods as they did in the early twentieth century. And, as then, there are new debates about what 'music' is and whether it can be credited to a bird.

In this new edition I have aired my own thoughts on these questions, fuelled by new listenings at home and abroad, and by discussions with biologists, some of whom are beginning to accept that there is more to a bird's singing than defending territory and attracting a mate – even if it is just satisfying its own pleasure centres. Alongside this we have the bird's rich and tangled cultural history – so revealing of our changing attitudes towards nature – through which I've tried to crawl, something like the poet John Clare as he stalked this mysterious, elusive creature: '... like a very boy/Creeping on hands and knees through matted thorns/To find her nest .../All seemed as hidden as a thought unborn.'

Richard Mabey

1

'All Elysium in a spot of ground'

from

The Flower and the Leaf

When she I sought, the nightingale, replied:
So sweet, so shrill, so variously she sung,
That the grove echoed, and the valleys rung;
And I so ravished with her heavenly note,
I stood entranced, and had no room for thought,
But all o'erpowered with ecstasy of bliss,
Was in a pleasing dream of paradise;
At length I waked, and looking round the bower
Searched every tree, and pried on every flower,
If anywhere by chance I might espy
The rural poet of the melody;
For still methought she sung not far away:
At last I found her on a laurel spray. . ..
On the green bank I sat, and listened long;
(Sitting was more convenient for the song:)
Nor till her lay was ended could I move,
But wished to dwell for ever in the grove.
Only methought the time too swiftly passed,
And every note I feared would be the last.
My sight, and smell, and hearing, were employed,
And all three senses in full gust enjoyed.
And what alone did all the rest surpass,
The sweet possession of the fairy place;
Single, and conscious to myself alone
Of pleasures to the excluded world unknown;
Pleasures which nowhere else were to be found,
And all Elysium in a spot of ground.

Anon, late fifteenth century,
adapted by John Dryden, 1700

It's early May, a nightingale moon. I'm perched in a narrow lane above the Stour Valley in Suffolk, listening to the birds. The landscape is already drained of colour, caught in that moment between light and dark when distances and outlines blur. I try to focus on the tumulus of scrub in front of me, but it seems to be dancing and flashing with phosphorescence. I know this is just my eyes playing tricks, but it gives the undergrowth an oddly insubstantial feel, quite out of keeping with the brilliant clarity of the song that is pouring from it.

It is my first nightingale of the year, and a coloratura into the bargain. It has a clipped, Latin style, full of deft phrases which are turned this way and that and drawn out into short, fading tremolos. As the moon rises, changing from hazy orange to platinum white, the singing becomes more assured. The sound is astonishingly pure and penetrating, broken with teasing, theatrical silences. I realize I am rooted to the spot, standing in the middle of the lane and barely noticing the cars edging past.

No other bird song can match these outpourings under the May full moon. Even by nightingale standards they seem more eloquent and passionate than at any other time of the spring. Perhaps this is just a flight of fancy on my part, a touch of moonshine. But it is a critical moment in the birds' year. Ever since early April nightingales have been migrating back to Europe from their wintering quarters in sub-tropical Africa, running the gauntlet of bird catchers and Mediterranean storms. The advance guard are almost all male birds, and since their arrival they will have been scouting out nesting territories in woodland thickets and river valleys. The females follow a week or so later, choosing warm, clear nights for migration if possible. These nights in early May mark the crescendo of the nightingales' courtship. Territories are settled, female birds are on the move and choosing mates, and the last waves of new arrivals are winging in. No wonder the males' songs seem so intense: they are serenades to tempt the females down from the sky.

Did Tennyson know about this when he wrote of how 'the music of the moon/Sleeps in the plain eggs of the nightingale'? The birds have always excited wild imaginings, and they have often lured me into wildly unexpected situations. This spring of all springs, I hadn't expected to be listening to them in the austere landscape of East Anglia. It was meant to be Portugal, with the woman in whose company I had trailed nightingales across northern Europe all the previous spring. Lily and I had planned to share our first birds of the year under the almond blossom in Alentejo. But the relationship faltered (plenty of singing but no shared territory) and we went our separate ways.

The spring after we parted was, as any good romantic is entitled to expect, dismal and pinching. Snow fell at Easter. The summer migrants were a whole month late. When the swifts finally arrived in early May – a thin, defiant arrow of birds careering in from the east as I was coming home from the shops – I was so relieved to see them that I drove the car into the kerb. But they proved to be the best of omens, and within two days England was suffused by exquisite, balmy weather. Having no stomach for moping alone by the Mediterranean, I sped to East Anglia, where I had first been bewitched by nightingales twenty years before.

Standing in this clamorous Suffolk lane, I don't feel it is that bad a swap. The moon is high enough to cast shadows now, and this virtuoso in front of me is unreeling my memories . . . South-west France, the previous June. The last nightingales of the year, up in a mist in the Corbières hills with Lily. Our very first nightingale together in the Dordogne, and the walnut liqueur we giggled our way through that evening in celebration. The year before that, and a miserable late April in the Provencal hilltop village of Les Baux. The mistral had blown for almost the whole week I was there, freezing out any hint of spring. Then, on the final day, I had woken to a brilliant sky and the sight of packs of alpine swifts hurtling round the medieval walls – and, down in the valley, the sound of a nightingale and hoopoe calling in concert.

The nightingale's song can do this, seeming frothy and funny one minute, then setting mundane puzzles – how does it utter some of those notes through a closed bill? – before plunging you again into resonant thickets of memory . . . this time of bad weather, and of brave stands made by the birds. Three singing into the teeth of an April gale from bushy shell-craters on the Tyneham military ranges in Dorset. A brave scattering on the last remnants of John Clare's Emmonsales Heath, in a gloomy May fog. An absurd, fleeting pang for a favourite cotton jumper I used to wear on cold evening vigils. Some lost struggles, too. Thirty-four nightingales found dead on a beach at Cadiz after a violent thunderstorm in April '91. And back home again that summer, empty woods, silent heaths and the realization that the bird is vanishing across much of its ancient habitation in central and southern England.

⸙⸙⸙⸙⸙⸙

There is a lull in the singing, a huge, emphatic silence that seems to be part of the performance. It is about 10 o'clock and the moon is almost at its height. By Suffolk standards I am on the top of the world. Below me, Arger Fen arches like a whaleback across the whole span of the southern horizon. Everywhere, dead elm stumps rear in silhouette amongst the scrub. The light is extraordinary – luminous, dusty, giving every pale surface the lustre of mother-of-pearl. Mounds of cow parsley and scythed grass glow in the moonbeams like suspended balls of mist. By the side of the lane I catch the scents of broom and bluebells, a blend of coconut and honey, the exotic and the homely, that has something of the ripened quality of the song itself.

I have wandered down the lane to a stream at the edge of the fen wood. There are bats hawking round the alders – silent, flickering shadows against the twigs. I wonder if a nightingale's high-tuned ears can pick up bats' squeakings? Do they register them, *attend* to them as we do to their songs?

At about 10.30, the silence is broken. The bird on the ridge has started up again, in the same patch of scrub as before. It's a quarter of a mile away, and this far off its song is almost percussive, like the sound of greenwood spitting in a fire. I begin to pick up other noises in the distance as I hurry back along the lane. A peacock, dogs, a tawny owl and a desultory, duller nightingale somewhere to the north, soon shamed into silence by this remarkable singer.

He is louder and more extravagant now, and seems to be rehearsing the whole nightingale repertoire. He sings a stylish four-note phrase, then repeats it in a minor key. He slides into a bubbling tremolo on a single note and holds it more than ten seconds. How does he breathe? I cannot believe he is not consciously improvising. I want to clap – and with barely credible timing, a shooting star arcs over the bush in which he is singing.

I am edging closer without realizing it and am now no more than ten feet away. Nothing stops the flow of notes. They fill the air, they seem to be solid, to be doing odd things to the light. I am half-aware that my peripheral vision is closing down, and that I am riveted to the bush by this tunnel of intense sound.

I remember Keats's enrapturement, and Shelley's lines 'Sounds overflow the listener's brain/So sweet, that joy is almost pain'. I draw back a little. But I can't sense any melancholy or anguish in my own response, only a slight sadness that I am listening to this stupendous performer on my own.

But the effort breaks the spell and I start to walk back to the car. The bird begins to recede, 'Past the near meadows, over the still stream,/Up the hill-side; and now 'tis buried deep . . .', and I am left, puzzling again over how another species, supposedly going about the routine business of defining its territory, can have such an extraordinary effect on one's senses and emotions.

2

'Immortal Bird'

from
Ode to a Nightingale

My heart aches, and a drowsy numbness pains
    My sense, as though of hemlock I had drunk,
Or emptied some dull opiate to the drains
    One minute past, and Lethe-wards had sunk:
'Tis not through envy of thy happy lot,
    But being too happy in thy happiness, –
        That thou, light-winged Dryad of the trees,
          In some melodious plot
    Of beechen green, and shadows numberless,
        Singest of summer in full-throated ease.

O, for a draught of vintage! that hath been
    Cool'd a long age in the deep-delved earth,
Tasting of Flora and the country green,
    Dance, and Provencal song, and sunburnt mirth!
O for a beaker full of the warm South,
    Full of the true, the blushful Hippocrene,
        With beaded bubbles winking at the brim,
          And purple-stained mouth;
    That I might drink, and leave the world unseen,
        And with thee fade away into the forest dim:

Fade far away, dissolve, and quite forget
    What thou amongst the leaves hast never known,
The weariness, the fever, and the fret
    Here, where men sit and hear each other groan;
Where palsy shakes a few, sad, last gray hairs,
    Where youth grows pale, and spectre-thin, and dies;
        Where but to think is to be full of sorrow
          And leaden-eyed despairs,
    Where Beauty cannot keep her lustrous eyes,
        Or new Love pine at them beyond to-morrow [. . .]

Darkling I listen; and, for many a time
　I have been half in love with easeful Death,
Call'd him soft names in many a mused rhyme,
　To take into the air my quiet breath;
Now more than ever seems it rich to die,
　To cease upon the midnight with no pain,
　　While thou art pouring forth thy soul abroad
　　　In such an ecstasy!
　Still wouldst thou sing, and I have ears in vain –
　To thy high requiem become a sod.

Thou wast not born for death, immortal Bird!
　No hungry generations tread thee down;
The voice I hear this passing night was heard
　In ancient days by emperor and clown:
Perhaps the self-same song that found a path
　Through the sad heart of Ruth, when, sick for home,
　　She stood in tears amid the alien corn;
　　　The same that oft-times hath
　Charm'd magic casements, opening on the foam
　Of perilous seas, in faery lands forlorn.

Forlorn! the very word is like a bell
　To toll me back from thee to my sole self!
Adieu! the fancy cannot cheat so well
　As she is fam'd to do, deceiving elf.
Adieu! adieu! thy plaintive anthem fades
　Past the near meadows, over the still stream,
　　Up the hill-side; and now 'tis buried deep
　　　In the next valley-glades:
　Was it a vision, or a waking dream?
　　Fled is that music: – Do I wake or sleep?

John Keats, 1819

W hen Keats called the nightingale the 'immortal Bird', he was talking of the way the bird's song seemed to transcend the individual, mortal singer, and how it had been an immemorial antidote to decay and grief. It is hard to think of another wild creature which has had such a revered and versatile role. At various times the nightingale has served as a kind of parish familiar or local wood spirit; as a symbol, and messenger, of love; as a harbinger of spring and an archetype of natural music. Aristophanes called it 'peerless in song'. In 630 CE, the monk Aldhelm of Malmesbury made it the subject of a riddle, that played on the irony of a small brown bird acquiring such a musical reputation: 'Mean is my colour but none hath scorned my song.'

It has long been the most versified bird in Western literature. To medieval French troubadours and German minnesingers, nightingales were emblems of spring and of love, both courtly and bawdy. In the thirteenth century they came to stand for the dawning mood of liberal humanism against the authoritarianism of the traditional Church, for fes-tiveness against puritanism. For early English writers, too, they were cheerful, engaging birds, the friends and confidants of lovers. In much of Renaissance Europe 'listening to the night-ingale' became a euphemism for sexual frolicking.

Then, for a few centuries, the mood changed. Influenced by a group of maudlin classical myths which had only a tangential connection with the real bird, pastoral poets began representing the nightingale's song as an outpouring of grief. Matthew Arnold's verse was one of the last gasps of this tradition, but also one of the most mawkish: 'That wild, unquench'd, deep-sunken, old-world pain . . . /How thick the bursts come crowding through the leaves!/Again – thou hearest!/Eternal passion!/Eternal Pain!'

But by this time the bird had already been recaptured by the Romantics, and become the subject of three of the great poems of the era – by Coleridge, Keats and John Clare. Each gave a quite different gloss to the song, but all three were inspired by real nightingales, and in their separate ways were united in a celebration of what they saw as the birds' joyous affirmation of life.

It has been a heavy burden of symbolism for a small bird to bear, and over the ages countless nightingales were all too liter-ally sacrificed for it. Guided by sympathetic magic ('like cures like'), their organs were used in love potions and in nostrums for improving the voice. In 1661 Robert Lovell recommended the bird's flesh as a remedy for sleepiness: 'The *flesh* is sweete and wholesome. It causeth watchfulnesse . . . The *gall* with honey cleareth the eyes.'

But the bird had more benign ways of encouraging watchfulness. Naturalists listened to it, observed its comings and goings, and had their own insights. In the seventeenth century it provided the evidence for the first theory linking bird song with nesting territory – and, three centuries later, for the realization that such elaborate performances must stand for a good deal more.

On occasions it has made whole parishes hold their breath for a season. The writer Garth Christian remembered a time in the 1930s when a stray pair were reported in the Golden Valley in Derbyshire, way outside their usual range. They were treated like prodigies:

> For a night or two the excitements of whippet racing and pigeon fancying were forgotten. Men listened earnestly and critically as they did when the parish choir performed *The Messiah*. Short tough colliers who had worked with D.H. Lawrence ('T'a young lad of 'is were a rum 'n, all brain an' not a deal of muscle'), men who shared a deep delight in Handel and strong beer, and real pride in the bullfinches they kept in tiny cages, crowded along the lane where the nightingale sang.

In Yorkshire an even more exceptional pair became such a local attraction that an enterprising bus firm started a 'Nightingale Special', ferrying passengers to the wood at sixpence a head. And in the 1920s, the Metropolitan Railway Company, attempting to create the first generation of commuters, focused one of its advertising campaigns around the bird's comforting presence at the end of the line:

> The song of the nightingales for which the
> neighbourhood is renowned; its gentle pastures, woods
> and streams; its gentle hills clothed with verdure,
> created by crops and thicket; the network of translucent
> rivers traversing the valley, render Rickmansworth a
> Mecca to the city man pining for country and pure air.

No wonder that other nocturnal singers are often transfigured into nightingales in the minds of hopeful listeners. Robins (the most common 'false nightingales'), for example, are apt to break into wistful song at any time of night and any time of year, especially in the warmth of towns. It may well have been a suburban robin that William Cowper, normally a perceptive observer of birds, described in his poem 'To the Nightingale, which the Author heard Sing on New Year's Day': 'Whence is it that, amazed, I hear/From yonder withr'd spray,/This foremost morn of all the year,/The melody of May?' (Nightingales sing in the daytime too, but are 6,000 miles away from Britain on New Year's Day.) And the night birds which have made Londoners pause in their strolls through Berkeley Square ever since Judy Campbell first sang the famous song at the height of the Blitz in 1940 have doubtless all been insomniac robins or blackbirds.

≈≈≈≈≈≈

But why the nightingale? Why not the robin or blackbird, or one of the summer warblers? They all have captivating songs, yet none of them has become such a source of inspiration and metaphor. Is the appeal of the nightingale's song simply self-fulfilling, with one generation of romantic associations and literary references shaping the next? Or does it have some intrinsic quality, some deep structure that reaches sympathetic depths in us?

It hardly needs spelling out that one source of the birds' power is their association with the night, and a way of life that seems imbued with secrecy. Their song apart, nightingales are among the least public of birds. They are subfusc, retiring, temporary. They come to Europe for just a few months each spring and sing for not much more than six weeks. This virtual dis-embodiment has helped make their song the equivalent of a psychologist's ink-blot test, capable of carrying all kinds of meaning, and has heightened its ambivalence. Yet it is more than this. The song has a compelling, mystifying, musical quality. It enchants most people who are prepared to listen, but makes us ask questions too, about what the bird is doing, how it is making choices about what to sing, whether it has some instinctive sense analogous to our own feelings for musicality. Many species – thrushes, blackcaps, skylarks – have tone and rhythm and melody, but nightingales have drama and narrative too, the extra resonance of *oratory*. With its crescendos and redolent pauses, the song hovers on the edge of dramatic monologue, of recitative. and I don't think it's far-fetched to describe the whole performance as operatic.

Oscar Wilde's poignant children's story 'The Nightingale and the Rose' hinges partly on this possibility, and on the question of whether a bird's song can be regarded as being on a par with human art. It also gathers together many of the images and conundrums that surround the bird. At its base is a widespread myth that first appears in early Iranian poetry, of a nightingale heightening the passion of its song by pressing its breast against a thorn, sometimes until it dies. (A stanza by the Iranian poet Hafiz goes: 'The nightingale with drops of his heart's blood/Had nourished the red rose, then came a wind/ And catching at the boughs in envious mood,/A hundred thorns about his heart entwined.')

In Wilde's story, the hero (for want of a better word) is a young philosophy student. He is languishing for a professor's daughter, who says she will dance with him at a ball if he brings her a red rose. But, he bewails, 'in all my garden there is no red rose.' A nightingale hears the student crying, and marvels. 'Here indeed is a true lover', he says. 'What I sing of, he suffers:

what is joy to me, to him is pain.' The bird decides to help but, on consulting the trees in the garden, finds that this will only be possible at a terrible cost. The rose tree, damaged by frost and gales, says that it can grow a red rose, but the nightingale 'must sing to me with your breast against a thorn. All night you must sing to me, and the thorn must pierce your heart, and your life-blood flow into my veins, and become mine.'

'Death is a great price to pay for a red rose,' the bird cries, but 'Love is better than Life, and what is the heart of a bird compared to the heart of a man?' So it resolves on its course of self-sacrifice and sings a farewell song for the oak tree in the garden, which is especially fond of the bird: 'I shall feel lonely when you are gone,' the oak remarks sadly.

The student overhears this performance and afterwards scribbles a criticism in his notebook. 'She [*sic* – poetic nightingales are often female] has form,' he says to himself, as he walks away through the grove, 'that cannot be denied to her; but has she got feeling? I am afraid not. In fact, she is like most artists; she is all style without any sincerity. She would not sacrifice herself for others. She thinks merely of music, and everybody knows that the arts are selfish. Still, it must be admitted that she has some beautiful notes in her voice. What a pity it is that they do not mean anything, or do any practical good!'

That night, under the moon, the nightingale flies to the rose tree and sings its heart out. And as it dies, so a single, exquisite red rose blooms on the tree.

'What a wonderful piece of luck,' cries the student. 'It is so beautiful that I am sure it has a long Latin name.' He picks the rose and carries it off to the professor's daughter. Alas, she rejects it. The colour will clash with her dress. Besides, the Chamberlain's nephew has already claimed her with a gift of red jewels. The rejected student storms off, hurls the rose into the gutter (where a cart runs over it) and returns to his books: 'What a silly thing Love is . . . it is always telling one of things that are not going to happen, and making one believe things that are not true . . . I shall go back to Philosophy and study Meta-physics.'

The twist Wilde gives to this story turns on its head one of the mainstays of bad Romantic writing: the idea that human emotions are sympathetically reflected in the natural world (the so-called Pathetic Fallacy). In Wilde's story, nature, in the shape of the nightingale, suffers by believing its hopes and feelings are reflected in *human* behaviour.

Wilde probably had other purposes in his story. Yet that shift of focus, from bird to human and back again, does open up a new way of looking at the mystery of the nightingale's appeal, and at what kind of communication is going on when we listen to its song. Most of the imaginative answers to this conundrum have been human-centred, and in essence have sought ways in which singing nightingales resemble humans.

They have looked at how closely the song approximates to music, at its capacity for absorbing – and conjuring up – memories and associations, at its power as a metaphor. Yet as far back as the medieval period there was another strand of writing which saw humans – poets and lovers especially – as a kind of nightingale. (Troubadour lyrics are full of jealousy over the superiority of nightingales as songsters.)

These days this viewpoint at least has more ecological respectability. It suggests, for instance, that the singing bird may be a kind of cultural ancestor, stirring primordial musical instincts, or ancient, common biological responses to place and season. It may even hint at a modern meaning for Romanticism, not in the patently absurd belief that nature feels human emotions, but that, at a basic level, all creatures share expressive feelings about the great pulses of their lives.

3

'A sort of sooty ball'

from
The Owl and the Nightingale

For when a man has finished the deed,
All his boldness begins to fade.
Once he has stung beneath the dress,
Then his love no longer lasts.
And so it is with your own mood:
As soon as you have started to brood,
Your song goes sour, your tune awry,
For you behave in the self-same way:
When you are done with all your vices,
Your voice begins to go to pieces.
But when the nights come hard and fast,
And bring the freezing winter frost,
Then for the first time it is seen –
Who is active, who is keen.
When days are bitter, then you find
Who goes forth, who lags behind . . .

Besides, you're filthy dark and small
Like a sort of sooty ball.
You have no loveliness or strength
And lack harmonious breadth and length.

Some of the Owl's arguments,
early thirteenth-century

The real bird behind this labyrinth of associations seems subdued to the point of disproportion. It is a cousin of the robin and little more than 6 inches long. Its plumage is largely brown, dull buff on the underparts with a russet back that becomes almost chestnut on the tail. It may not even be a very ancient species, and probably evolved separately from its closest relative, the thrush-nightingale, no more than 20,000 years ago. Now it breeds across the warmer parts of Europe and Central Asia, from Portugal and North Africa in the west to Mongolia in the east, with southern Denmark marking its most northerly outpost. Its breeding range is influenced by climate, and it is more or less confined to areas where the mean July temperature lies between 17 and 30°C. In Britain this means that nightingales have never nested in any numbers north and west of a line between Yorkshire and Dorset, and rarely above an altitude of about 600 feet. There are no records at all of breeding in west Wales, Ireland, or, unassisted, in Scotland. (Though in the mid-nineteenth century Sir John Sinclair tried unsuccessfully to introduce them by filling robins' nests with eggs pilfered from the London area. The young nightingales hatched, flew to Africa in autumn and sensibly never returned.) Their sensitivity to temperature isn't easily explained by their food preferences, as it is with some summer migrants. They take very few aerial insects (many of which fly only when the weather is warm) and feed instead largely on the ground, taking ants, small beetles and occasional spiders, worms and moth larvae. In late summer they will eat fruit, especially wild strawberries and elderberries. They are essentially foragers and move about the undergrowth in long hops, pausing frequently and tilting their heads on one side to listen for prey, in the same engaging way as robins.

They build their nests low in the bush layer, too, usually in a tangle of twigs and shoots, and rarely more than a foot above the ground. The nest seems like an extension of the undergrowth and is woven out of dry grass, some moss and feathers, and quantities of dead leaves, especially oak leaves. The nest-building is done exclusively by the female, who is also responsible for incubating the four or five mottled brown eggs. This leaves the male free to concentrate on territorial singing. But as soon as the young are hatched (in about thirteen days) he joins in feeding them and virtually ceases to sing. The only noises normally heard from nightingales after this are the rather undignified raspberries that serve as their alarm call, and which are also uttered from deep cover.

They are distributed widely across Europe and Asia, though their native habitat always includes dense scrub. In the Netherlands, they haunt the coastal sand dunes and the willow carr around the polders. In southern Russia, they breed in open hornbeam and alder woods and thickets of sea-buckthorn. The Asian race frequents orchards with little more than rough grass growing under the trees. In southern Spain they are common in cork-oak scrub, and in bramble and heather clumps in open pinewoods.

The warmer the conditions, the less fussy they are about their habitat. In the Mediterranean area there is almost no kind of vaguely bushy growth in which they don't occur. I have heard them in tiny village gardens in Majorca, in the formal shrubberies of the Alhambra Palace in Granada, on the edges of remote hillside meadows in Crete, and in Provence almost everywhere: in patches of giant reed and tamarisk at the edge of the Camargue rice-fields, in vineyard windbreaks and vine-yards gone wild. No one knows the world population, but there are more than a million pairs in France alone.

Nightingales also choose deep cover to sing from, though occasionally they will climb up to an exposed branch. (I once rather unkindly egged a nightingale into a very public decla-mation by playing its own song back to it from a tape recorder. It climbed to the top of a hawthorn twig to sing, so that I could watch the opening and shutting of its bill, which seemed in no way coordinated with the notes that were emerging from it.) As well as their full-blooded territorial recitals, most often delivered at night, they have shorter daytime songs aimed at approaching rivals, quiet courtship songs and more fragmentary calls for contacting the hen bird inside their territory, which say, it seems, 'Here I am. Where are you?'

In 1929 the pioneering bird photographer Emma Turner watched a male at close quarters for more than a week. 'I have never seen a bird so brimful of emotion,' she wrote. 'On the day the young hatched the male only brought food. Each time he visited his brooding mate he sang such a song as I had never heard before. His beak was full of juicy grubs for the family but this did not hinder him from pouring out a stream of liquid bubbling notes so soft and sweet that they were inaudible six feet away.'

The full territorial songs can sometimes turn into marathon performances. One bird was recorded as singing for twenty-three and a half hours in a single day. Separate spells of singing usually last between five and thirty minutes and are broken up into phrases of two to four seconds, with slightly shorter silences between. The phrases are hugely diverse (individual birds may have many hundreds in their vocabulary), but are always roughly similar in structure. There is a flourish of piping notes to begin with, sometimes in triplets or short arpeggios, and often with an urgent, whiplash quality; then a single note repeated as a rich, liquid bubbling or chuckling or slow trill, which in different phrases occurs at different pitches and speeds. The most extreme variation on this structure is so distinctive as to be almost the bird's signature tune. It is a sequence of long, sighing, indrawn whistles, mounting in crescendo on a single note until they fall, dramatically, to a deep rattle. These are the 'sweet, sweet, sweet, jug, jug' notes of so many poems (Coleridge's for example: 'And murmurs musical and swift jug jug,/And one low piping sound more sweet than all . . .').

Like other birds, it seems as if nightingales are born with an instinctive appreciation of the kind of song they 'ought' to sing, its structure, tonality and overall 'jizz' (the quality that makes it possible to identify a bird – or a person for that matter – from a fragment of behaviour or presentation). An individual bird then builds up its vocabulary by listening to its male parent and to other singing males. It may occasionally mimic phrases from other birds, especially blackcaps and thrushes. I have heard an otherwise rather subdued bird in Spain repeat a thrush-like couplet twice, exactly as a song thrush might; and another in Suffolk apparently so pleased with a more conventional nightingale phrase that he ran through it four times in succession. (John Clare once heard the converse of this, a thrush learning phrases from a nightingale: 'the little thrush that commenced singing in April sung till the middle of July & that he had got many variations from the nightingale in the last month which he did not commence with in April.') But this is a scarce occurrence and always has the feel of a deliberate choice by the bird, rather than the kind of occasional repetition that comes from the random shuffling of phrases. If it happened more often, the nightingale might not be regarded as such a 'good' singer.

We are back with the conundrum at the centre of the nightingale's story. The phrase 'good singer' trips off the tongue, but what exactly does it mean? Presumably we mean sounds good to us – strong, inventive, *musical*. But how does it sound to other nightingales, the only intended audience? Are we assuming our critical criteria are the same as the birds'? Might there be other more subtle qualities in the song, indicators, say, of well-being, loyalty, pleasure, even good company, that we are deaf to? And might birds also have a kind of aesthetic sense, different from but sometimes chiming with our own?

Sound communication is not qualitatively all of a piece. Voices (of any creatures) convey more, in terms of information and emotion, than coincidental natural noise – the sounds of breathing or eating, for instance. Bird calls convey more than the unvarying chirps of insects, and bird songs more than the curt messages carried by contact and alarm calls. Caught somewhere between chance euphony – the rustle of a southerly breeze in the trees – and deliberate, abstracted music, they are full of evolutionary possibility. Perhaps they contain within them the template for our own musical sense.

As for the nightingale's song, it seems to hover on the edge of speech, of dramatic oratory. This is the sense that H.E. Bates caught, in what I think is the most evocative of all prose descriptions of the song:

It has some kind of electric, suspended quality that has a far deeper beauty than the most passionate of its sweetness. It is a performance made up, very often, more of silence than of utterance. The very silences have a kind of passion in them, a sense of breathlessness and restraint, of restraint about to be magically broken. It can be curiously seductive and maddening, the song beginning very often by a sudden low chucking, a kind of plucking of strings, a sort of tuning up, then flaring out in a moment: into a crescendo of fire and honey and then, abruptly, cut off again in the very middle of the phrase. And then comes that long, suspended wait for the phrase to be taken up again, the breathless hushed interval that is so beautiful. And often, when it is taken up again, it is not that same phrase at all, but something utterly different, a high sweet whistling prolonged and prolonged for the sheer joy of it, or another trill, or the chuck-chucking beginning all over again.

4

'Most melancholy bird'

'A Prediction'

Our Host had three Nightingales, placed separately, so that
each was shut up singly by itself in a dark Cage. It happened
that at that time, being the Spring of the year, when those
birds are wont to sing indefatigably, and almost incessantly;
I was so afflicted with the Stone, that I could sleep but very
little all night. Then about and after Midnight, where there
was no noise in the house, but all still, you might have heard
strange janglings and emulations of two Nightingales,
talking one with another, and plainly imitating men's
discourses. For my part I was almost astonished with wonder.
For they in the night-season, when all was whist and quiet, in
conference together produced and repeated whatever they
had heard in the day time from the Guests talking together,
and had thought upon . . . it is wonderful to tell, how they
provoked one another, and by answering invited and drew
one another to speak. Yet did they not confound their words,
talking both together, but rather utter them alternately, or by
course . . . a History or Prediction of the War of the
Emperour against the Protestants, which was then inuninent.
For as it were presaging or prophecying they seemed to chant
forth the whole business as it afterwards fell out. They did
also with that story mingle what had been done before
against the Duke of Brunswick. But I suppose those Birds
had all from the secret conference of some Noblemen and
Captains, which as being in a public Inn, might frequently
have been had in that place where the Birds were kept.

Konrad von Gesner,
quoted by Francis Willughby,
in *The Ornithology,* 1628

M any of the scientific accounts of nightingale songs are distant and reductionist, as if they were describing a string of random Morse code signals or a test exercise on a musical instrument. There is no sense that the structure of the song might have as much significance as the vehemence of its delivery. Perhaps this is because many of the nightingales so studied were in cages, which invariably imprison the imagination of the listener as much as they do the bird.

Caged nightingales were popular at least as far back as the Roman Empire, and were looked on as a kind of status symbol. Pliny (in 77 CE) remarks that the best singers could fetch the kind of prices normally given for slaves:

A bird not in the lowest rank remarkable. In the first place there is so loud a voice and so persistent a supply of breath in such a tiny little body; then there is the consummate knowledge of music in a single bird: the sound is given out with modulations, and now is drawn out into a long note with one continuous breath, now made staccato by checking it, or linked together by prolonging it, or carried on by holding it back; or it is suddenly lowered, and at times sinks into a mere murmur, loud, low, bass, treble, with trills, long notes, modulated when this seems good – soprano, mezzo, baritone; and briefly all the devices in that tiny throat which human science has devised with all the elaborate mechanisms of the flute.

Fifteen hundred years later Pliny's fellow-countryman Olina became the first naturalist to realize the connection between bird song and assertion of territory. It was, he suggested, 'proper' to the nightingale, 'at his first coming to occupy or seize upon one place as its freehold, into which it will not admit any other nightingale but its mate'. He was, as it turned out, quite correct. But his scientific credibility on this point was hardly helped by the fact that he occasionally rooted birds to the spot with an 'odoriferous unguent'.

'As the Nightingale exceeds all other birds in singing, so doth he also in the exquisiteness of his scent,' he wrote. So:

Take of Civet not sophisticate twenty grains, Benjamin and Storax calamite, of each three grains, mingle these together in a Mortar in the form of an ointment; Then diligently observe the bush and particular branch, on which the Nightingale is wont to sit and sing, and there making as it were a little shelf of the leaves and boughs, lay thereon four meal-worms, and anoint the branch next to your shelf with this Unguent. The Nightingale when he returns from feeding, will presently fly up to his bough, and finding there the meal-worms will fall a eating of them, and scenting the odour of the Ointment will begin to sing, and being as it were intoxicated with the perfume, will not give over, nor stir from the place though you take the boughs from about him.

Even eighteenth-century naturalists had few qualms about catching the birds. Daines Barrington, one of Gilbert White's correspondents, had the renowned surgeon John Hunter dissect large numbers of songbirds and discovered that those with the 'best' voices had the strongest and most developed syrinxes (birds' voice boxes: each individual has two). The nightingale's was larger than that of any bird of comparable size. The popular natural history painter Eleazar Albin had a seemingly more tender attitude, and was fulsome in his praise of bird musicianship. In *A Natural History of British Song-birds* (1737) he writes:

The Animal World does not afford more agreeable
Objects to the Eyes, nor none that so sweetly gratifies
the Sense of Hearing. They were undoubtedly
designed by the Great Author of Nature, on Purpose
to entertain and delight Mankind, who for their
Generosity are well pleased with these pretty
innocent Creatures.

But he was also a creature of his time, and couldn't see beyond
the image of songbirds as divine toys for human entertainment.
He continues: 'I could not do a more acceptable service for the
Lovers of these sweet Choristers of the Woods, than to instruct
how to catch and keep them.'

His instructions on procuring and training reliable domes-
tic nightingales are a long way removed from his earlier
blandishments. He insists that they should be taken before they
have fledged. They should be fed with 'sheep's Heart, or other
Flesh Meat raw, chopped very fine . . . well cleansed and freed
from Skin, sinews, and Fat or Strings, which will be apt to stick
in their Throats, or twine about their Tongues . . .' He reckoned
they could become 'fat and foggy' in autumn (when they should
be fed spiders) and 'gouty' if kept for long periods in a cage.

John Bingley, in *Animal Biography* (1802), went one stage
further in praising the accomplishments of the 'Choristers of the
Woods'. He drew up a league table of the 'comparative merits of
the singing-birds of our own island', scored as if they were com-
peting in a village fete. He awarded seventeen species marks out

of twenty for five qualities. The nightingale wins, scoring nineteen for 'mellowness of tone', fourteen for 'sprightliness', and nineteen each for 'plaintiveness', 'compass' and 'execution'. The robin was awarded respectively 6, 16, 12, 12, 12, and the linnet 12, 16, 12, 16, 18. There are some. curious anomalies in Bingley's list, symptoms perhaps of the taste of the times. The blackbird's languorous song for instance, wins just four for mellowness and nothing at all for plaintiveness; and the dunnock's, which these days would be regarded as one of the most cheerful of hedgerow jingles, gets nought for sprightliness.

Bingley was another keeper of caged nightingales and he passes on stories of the quirks and performances he has either heard or heard about. If humans play or sing to them they can be taught to whistle in tune or in time and will spontaneously modulate their key if necessary. They can even be persuaded to join in 'choruses . . . and to repeat their couplet at the proper time'.

The life expectations (and probably the songs) of the majority of hapless nightingales caught to adorn bird fanciers' parlours were dismal. In 1867 James Harting logged the bags of three professional catchers in outer London, and found that between 13 April and 2 May they took 225 birds, all but six of them male. The techniques of the trappers who used to loot the Surrey woods (then believed to house the best songsters) were described in grisly detail by Richard Jefferies in 1886:

In the 'good old days of bird-catching' it was child's play to snare them. A couple of roughs would come down from town and silence a whole grove. The nightingale would watch the trap being laid, and pounce on the alluring meal-worm as soon as the trapper was out of sight. It would be quite as much curiosity as gluttony that led to its fate; and the fate was a sad one. These birds are so shy that it is nearly impossible to keep them alive. They literally beat themselves to death against their prison wires. So for the first fortnight of captivity the wings were tied, and the bird was kept caged in the dark. Light was gradually let in – at first by a few pinholes in the paper that covered the cage. The captive would peck and peck at these until a rent was made and in time the paper could come away. The mortality was pitiable. Seventy percent of these little creatures that were singing a week before in full-throated ease in the Surrey lanes would be flung out into the gutters of Seven Dials or Whitechapel.

A succession of bird protection acts, beginning in 1880, has largely put a stop to this sordid trade. But nightingales are still caught and reared in captivity, and still experimented with. In 1992 two behavioural zoologists at the Free University of Berlin caught and isolated nightingale nestlings and then 'tutored' them by playing tapes of bird song. They found that the birds could often repeat complex sequences of up to sixty different phrases after hearing them once a day for two or three weeks. During the experiment they discovered a good deal about how nightingales learned new material and stored it in different memory layers. (Their short-term memory alone can accommodate seven song sequences, each nearly a minute long.)

But it's as well not to extrapolate too much from the behaviour of captive nightingales. All imprisoned creatures behave differently from their cousins in the wild. They lack the social context of mate and offspring, and the rich constantly varying stimuli of a natural environment. Most of all they are moulded by the relationships they have with their keepers and the reward systems they have established.

The remarkable story of the ventriloquial nightingales quoted at the beginning of this chapter was recounted by the seventeenth-century ornithologist Francis Willughby. It concerned an experience of a friend of the German scientist Konrad von Gesner, who was attending the Diet at Ratisbone in 1546, and staying at 'a common Inn at the sign of the Golden Crown'. The narrator is sceptical at first of the birds' facility for 'imitating men's discourses', and asks his host whether the birds' tongues have been slit, or if they have been deliberately taught. The host answers no, and denies any knowledge of the birds' nocturnal conversations. But the guest, not able to sleep because of illness, continues to be entertained by the birds' apparent gossip. He hears tales of the continuing rows between a tapster and his wife, repeated in all their original, unexpurgated detail ('And if by chance in their wrangling they cast forth any unseemly words, and that ought rather to have been suppressed and kept secret, the Birds, not knowing the difference between modest and immodest, honest and filthy words, did out with them.') And, most bizarrely, they also uttered 'a History or Prediction of the War of the Emperour against the Protestants, which was then imminent'. (Charles V declared war on 26 June 1546.)

It is hard to understand what was really going on during those nights at Ratisbone. Perhaps the whole thing was just the fantasy of an ill and possibly intoxicated insomniac. Perhaps, like Keats's Ruth, he was also 'sick for home'. Or perhaps the narrator was making a veiled political or religious point. Given the nightingale's reputation as a catalyst for the imagination, it might even be an early urban myth.

5

'The happiest part of summers fame . . .'

A Riddle

I talk through my mouth with many tongues,
Vary my tone, and often change
The sound of my voice. I give loud cries,
Keep my tune, make songs without ceasing.
An old evening singer, I bring pleasure
To people in towns. When I burst
Into a storm of notes, they fall silent,
Suddenly listening. Say what I'm called
Who like a mimic loudly mock
A player's song, and announce to the world
Many things that are welcome to men.

Anon, probably eighth century

The nightingale's song is so hedged about with associations that it is hard to say if there is anything intrinsically captivating about it. Did it turn the heads of prehistoric humans? Do young children notice it, unprompted? I have no recollection of hearing nightingales when I was a child, but suspect I must have done. By all accounts the birds were common enough in the Chiltern woods and heaths I haunted in the late 1940s and 1950s. I knew a few birds' songs, especially ones that were rhythmic enough to imitate. I could recognize – and just about whistle back – the green woodpecker's 'yaffle' and the yellowhammer's 'little bit of bread and no cheese'. And, with an expectant, half-formed sense that they were portents of the spring, I learned to listen out for the songs of returning warblers. But either the nightingales were somewhere else, or their sophisticated phrases failed to connect with the pre-occupations of a juvenile birdwatcher.

Children's responses may depend on the context in which they hear the bird. When he was little more than five years old, Coleridge's son, Hartley, could already recognize – and apparently relish – the Quantock birds that his father was to celebrate in one of the great nightingale poems.

> How he would place his hand beside his ear,
> His little hand, the small forefinger up,
> And bid us listen!

The young son of my late East Anglian friend Roger Deakin also benefited from his father's enthusiasm for the bird. When he was seven years old he read Roald Dahl's story *Danny, the Champion of the World* and developed a desperate desire to try his hand at poaching. Roger, not wanting to squash his interest, suggested they hunted nightingales with a tape recorder rather than pheasants with a gun, and they spent an enchanted night together in the Suffolk woods. (When he was much older Roger's son returned the compliment by 'arranging' the song they recorded that night as part of an answerphone message.)

The young Gertrude Jekyll, on the other hand, became tetchy about the sheer torrent of nightingale song that anyone living in the Surrey woods was subject to in the nineteenth century. One morning, when she was in her early teens, she came down to breakfast without boots. Asked by her parents to explain, she said she had hurled them at the nightingales carolling ceaselessly outside her bedroom.

Max Ernst's surrealist picture-relief *Two Children are Threatened by a Nightingale* (1924) relies for much of its effect on the benign, or at least ingenuous, views children normally have of songbirds; only in the most disorientating kind of nightmare could a nightingale possibly seem *threatening*. But Ernst's piece is precisely of a dream full of irrationality and menace. Across a landscape hemmed in by a wall, two figures flee from a hovering nightingale no bigger than a speck in the vast sky. A girl, holding what seems to be a dagger in her hand, is running either towards the bird or towards a wooden gate which is hinged to the frame of the work. A male figure, holding another small girl in his arms, leaps along the roof of a tiny, windowless house. He is reaching out into the real world, towards an alarm bell, which is also fixed to the frame. A fourth figure lies prostrate by the side of the house.

It is a disruptive and unsettling picture, but would be equally so if the 'threatening' creature were a wren or a butterfly. Given that the Freudian theory of dreams was one of the chief inspirations of Surrealism, the deliberate naming of the minute bird in Ernst's picture as a nightingale may be a reference to its tradition as a symbol – and inciter – of sexual liaisons, an avian aphrodisiac provoking mayhem among the innocent.

But that is one of the more sophisticated nightingale associations, and a comparatively late arrival in the bird's cultural history – just as it is in most listeners' lives. For most of us, I suspect, the songs of particular birds stand for more homely and personal memories. They can be as evocative as smells for conjuring up places, holidays, friendships, love affairs and, especially, moments of the year. An early blackbird song can still summon up for me the mood and aura of a particular moment in my childhood. It is an early evening in late March, the clocks have just been put forward and there is a warm southerly breeze. It is the first day our back door is left open after tea, joining the house with the garden again. And soon I am sitting out there, listening to the rambling monologue from the top of our lilac tree.

If the blackbird's song was the first I remember, the swift's was the first I deliberately sought out. From May onwards the packs screamed round the school hall and the parish church where our choir sang motets through the summer. They were good-luck charms for me, and I used to trudge up to cricket at the start of the summer term, clutching my blazer collar and fervently hoping that I would catch my first glimpse of those careering crescent wings on the first day of May.

When, a little older, I became a more serious bird watcher, the chiffchaff became my talisman, and its song a sure sign that the Easter holidays had begun. But the ritual of combing the local woods for the first arrival was as much a competitive game as a celebration of spring, and my chief aim was to push my personal date as far as possible back into March. I had read somewhere that the first waves of migrants reached this country 'as promptly as if they were following an airline timetable'. Chiffchaffs came on 16 March, followed by willow warblers on the 21st. I was amazed at the thought of these diminutive creatures making their 5,000-mile journeys with such precision, and longed to hear one on its 'proper' date.

Even then there was something that touched me about the chiffchaff's optimistic, see-saw note, drifting down from the top of a leafless ash tree. I learned that chiffchaffs were individuals and did not all sound like metronomes. Their songs were often relaxed, loose-rhythmed, slurred. I heard one bird which always sang a pure triplet – chiff-*chaff*-chiff; another whose song was pared down to a minimalist chiff-chiff.

In late autumn the first fieldfare flocks would arrive from Scandinavia. I would often hear them, sounding like the clacking of distant castanets, as they passed high overhead in the early morning; or late in a November afternoon, shuttling in invisible, nomadic bands through the gathering mist. Without fail their southerly flights were followed within two or three days by the first bad weather of the winter.

Much later in my life, bird songs began to be emblems for particular habitats. The bubbling sound of the curlew still conjures up Yorkshire Dales hay-meadows in May, and the piping three-note whistle of the greenshank – as pure and powerful in its own way as the opening bars of a nightingale's song – evokes the Norfolk marshes in late summer. The scratches and churrs of grasshopper warblers, turtle doves, nightjars and whitethroats seem perfectly suited to the scruffy, spiny cover of their favourite heathland habitats. The whitethroat's bramble-patch style even extends to its song flight, which Gilbert White described as a series of 'odd jerks and gesticulations over the hedges and bushes'.

I understood just how deeply these songs were impacted with particular places when, one summer when I was in my early thirties, they began to fade. I thought at first that there had simply been another warbler slump, until I realized the swift packs were also silent and that almost all other birds seemed to have receded into the distance. I had, it turned out, premature high-tone hearing loss. I doubt if I will hear swifts unaided again, or the flourish at the end of a wren's song, or the full tumult of a dawn chorus. But a modern hearing aid has restored virtually everything else and brought, thank goodness, the blackbirds back into the garden. And more recently I have acquired a bird song equivalent of a bat detector, which transposes songs down into lower registers without changing the pace or rhythm. The resulting soundscape of whoops and glissandi and previously unnoticed grace notes makes me wonder if this is how birds hear each other's songs.

I think this experience, of the loss of what amounted to part of my sense of place, may have been responsible for an odd, compensatory belief I nurtured for a while. So many bird songs seemed to me to 'fit' a landscape, to be scored as evocatively as pieces of programme music, that I wondered if it was an ecological adaptation, the sound equivalent of camouflage. Put like that, of course, it was an absurd, anthropomorphic fantasy: landscape 'character' is a human construct which bird song helps to shape, rather than being shaped by it.

Yet there may have been a grain of truth in my notion. Birds which frequent similar habitats do have similar qualities in their songs and calls. Birds of open spaces, for example, can rely on visual signals and convey messages by plumage or display flights. Their songs tend to be short and uncomplicated. Birds of dense woodland, on the other hand, need to place more emphasis on sound for communication and advertisement, and their songs are often more elaborate and far-reaching. This seems to hold true whether the wood in question is a rain forest or an English copse. Edward Armstrong, an early Cambridge ornithologist, gave a graphic account of how he was struck by homesickness on hearing the bird songs of the Amazonian jungle:

> The clanging note of the bell-bird of the South
> American forest stirs the emotions – for a moment the
> surprised wayfarer is transported by the bell-note out
> of the wilderness to the Sunday calm of an English
> hamlet. Almost simultaneously, conscious of the
> enveloping rain forest, disillusionment and a sense of
> desolation assail him.

Nightingales came into my life rather late, at a time when I was more interested in adding new birds to my list than in looking for romantic associations. My first encounter with the bird was in such incongruous circumstances as to be almost comic. I was up on the north Norfolk coast in the late 1960s, rediscovering bird-watching with an old friend. We had spent most of our time down on the salt marshes, poking about in the creeks and watching the spring passage of wading birds *en route* from Africa to their breeding grounds. It was a feast of first encounters for us: black-tailed godwits mobbing Montagu's harriers, ruff in such gaudily varied summer plumage that we thought they were all different species, and urgent flocks of dunlin and golden plover, bound for the northern tundra. We made shameless lists of first-time birds, birds seen in a day, birds 'possibly seen'.

One morning we struck inland on the trail of the red-backed shrikes that nested regularly on Salthouse Heath about a mile from the coast. We'd been told roughly where they were to be found, in a patch of thorn scrub by a grassy clearing that served as a parking space. We duly parked the car and waited. The day was drab and overcast, and there was no sign of the shrikes. Robins and willow warblers tried out brief, fitful phrases and then fell silent. It was the kind of day for moping in a bush, or a car. But just before noon, out of the blackthorn – though seemingly out of nowhere – came a burst of glass-clear notes that jolted us out of our torpor. Neither of us had heard a nightingale before, but we knew instantly what it must be. It was the power and tone of the song that was so striking. It seemed ridiculously loud for this little heathland enclave, almost theatrically projected, as if a migrant wader from the marsh had set down in a bush and begun calling for company.

Soon this first bird was joined by a second, singing from the opposite side of the clearing, and for twenty minutes we sat enthralled while they duelled across us, swapping phrases, shouting each other down, at times linked in what seemed like a musical round. And as potent as the phrases themselves were the cliff-hanging silences that punctuated them, and which I was to learn were one of the key elements of the bird's perform-ance, as if it were deliberately leaving space for a reply.

I heard and remember all this, but cannot recall being stirred to passion or melancholy or any of the emotions sup-posedly aroused by, or contained in, the nightingale's song. All I recollect about my reactions when that first stream of notes flared out is erupting with a rash of sympathetic gooseflesh. It was a *sensual* experience. The whole performance, at that unpromising spot and time, was like taking an exotic cocktail with elevenses.

I didn't come across many more nightingales for the next few years, but that Norfolk experience proved to be more than a chance meeting. I realized that, in East Anglia at least, the birds had a particular liking for dense scrub near grassy clear-ings, and I became a connoisseur of rural car-park performers. It grew to be something of a party trick. I would draw up non-chalantly in a likely lay-by in May or early June, bet myself or my companion that a nightingale was there and simply wait for it to start up. I usually won my bet, though I am not terribly proud to admit it. I think I did pick up a vague and instinctive sense of the kind of place nightingales haunted (and a knack of identifying their song a long way off from just a couple of notes). But these auditions were really just showing off, a kind of territorial display of my own, and it was years before I found any subtler resonances in the song. In those early days the nightingale's song simply meant the open heaths, the English bush and those enticingly warm, muddled scrublands of the south country. I look back now and can scarcely credit how frequent, how accessible they were half a century ago.

⸎⸎⸎⸎⸎⸎

The bush may be the oldest association of all, and perhaps the bird's aboriginal home. At the height of the most recent ice age, nightingales may not have been migratory birds. They may have spent the whole year in the savanna, the open scrubland which then covered much of the African continent. But as the ice retreated from northern Europe, the African interior began to warm up and it's possible that this prompted the regular seasonal escapes to more bearable temperatures that eventually became the habit of migration. The nightingale arrived in Britain, to judge from the few fossils that have been found, about 10,000 years ago.

It is hard to imagine them being ignored by early people in northern Europe. They were key players in the great annual change-round of birds each spring. One week there would be flocks of wild duck and geese on the wetlands, and the next packs of swifts screaming round the crags and countless small birds piping in the undergrowth. More often than not, the arrival of these summer migrants would coincide with spells of fine weather, and they must have been looked on as good omens.

Even then, nightingales would have stood out as something remarkable, the loudest and most tantalizingly secretive of the newcomers. Did people try to mimic them, hoping that, by sympathetic magic, a few reverently echoed phrases might guarantee more of those hunters' full moons under which the song was so often heard?

It's also likely that nightingales became a kind of village familiar in the Neolithic period, drawn to the edges of human settlements for the scrubland that followed forest clearance. In truly natural conditions (in northern Europe, at least) this kind of scrub woodland is quite scarce. It was abundant just after the retreat of the ice, but the climate then was too cool for there to be any nightingales to enjoy it. And when the temperatures did improve and the climax forest became established, scrub largely retreated to open, disturbed areas like flood-plains. It would flourish for a while where big trees had died and fallen, or where there had been forest fires, but vanish again as the woodland regenerated.

The arrival of the first farmers gave scrub its big boost. By clearing woodland for settlements and regularly and deliberately cropping or coppicing trees to provide building materials and fuel (a practice which had almost certainly begun by 4000 BCE in Britain), they created exactly the kind of bushy regrowth that has perennially attracted nightingales.

This was an association that flourished for as long as the practice of coppicing itself remained a common way of managing woodland. Coppicing relies on the ability of most of our native deciduous trees to sprout sheaves of bushy new poles if they are regularly cut back to ground level. Woods were usually cut on a rotation of between ten and fifteen years, and during cuts the compartments developed into dense shrubberies. As a commercial practice, coppicing became largely obsolete in Britain after the Second World War, though in a number of ancient woods coppicing has been reintroduced for nature conservation or amenity reasons. But nightingales don't use coppice woods indiscriminately. A survey in Kent at the beginning of the 1970s showed that their concentrations reach a peak five to eight years after the coppice is cut and fall away dramatically after ten years. Many similar studies since, in Suffolk, Essex, Oxfordshire and Worcestershire, for instance, have confirmed this finding. Nightingales like the density of vegetation in middle-aged coppicewood. It is tall and thick enough to provide good cover, but not so dark that the lower undergrowth – of honeysuckle, bramble, blackthorn, perhaps – is shaded out. They also seem to prefer an intimate mix of coppice species – ash, maple, hazel and oak, for example – and a scatter of uncut, standard trees amongst the bushy underwood. This may be because such trees provide denser areas of leaf-litter for feeding, or because low, tangled vegetation can persist for longer under their dappled shade than under the very dark cover of mature coppice.

There is much that is still mysterious about nightingales' habitat preferences. They will not nest regularly, for instance, in coppices where less than about seven to eight acres is cut each year. In some woods they will nest in free-growing areas and ignore the regularly cut plots, which may be connected with the browsing away of young coppice growth by deer in unfenced woods. And the reinstatement of coppicing at former nesting sites does not guarantee that nightingales will return. It may be that they have a strong loyalty to traditional nesting spots and won't colonize new areas readily, especially when these are some way from the places in which they were hatched and reared.

Coppice woodland seems generally to have become less attractive to nightingales. In central and eastern England they are more likely to be found in heaths and commons, river valleys and the scrubby margins of lakes and reservoirs. But these bushy habitats are themselves in decline. Many local authorities, farmers and even some conservation bodies have a revulsion for scrub, which they view as untidy, sterile and, mistakenly, of suppressing 'real' woodland.

So the nightingale, the hermit of the badlands, is ironically suffering from the ill-deserved reputation of its favourite retreat.

6

'The voluptuous nightingales . . .'

Song

Sweet Philomell in groaves and desarts haunting,
Oft glads my hart and eares with her sweet chaunting,
   But then her tunes delight me best,
   When pearcht with prick against her breast,
She sings fie, fie, fie, fie, as if she suffered wrong,
Till seeming pleas'd sweet, sweet concludes her song.

Sweet Jinny sings and talkes and sweetly smileth,
And with her wanton mirth my griefes beguileth:
   But then me thinkes she pleaseth best,
   When, while my hands move loves request,
She cries phy, phy, phy, phy, and seeming loath gainsaies,
Till better pleas'd sweet, sweet content bewrayes.

Anon, sixteenth-century

Set by Robert Jones, *The First Book of Songs or Ayres*

The idea of 'the bush' – the thicket, the secret trysting ground, the hidden retreat – runs like a leitmotif through the nightingale's story. It is one of the natural links between the bird's ecology and its place in romantic poetry, paralleling its real and metaphorical associations with the spring (incidentally an old English word for a bushy coppice).

But as far back as classical times, literary nightingales have been carriers of ideas which don't obviously echo features of the real bird's life. Paramountly they have been birds of love and passion – platonic, flirtatious; promiscuous love and, especially, rejected or hopeless love. To some extent this last association may have been fuelled by the 'sobbing' quality which some listeners hear in the song. But its literary origins lie in a widespread and exceptionally grisly classical myth, in which there is a magically 'sympathetic' transformation of a victim of violent distonguing into a bird with wondrous vocal powers.

The myth recounts the fate and metamorphosis of two sisters, Procne and Philomel. Procne is married to Tereus, king of Thrace, who rapes Philomel and then imprisons her, cutting out her tongue for good measure so that she cannot tell tales. Ovid's version of *c*.10 BCE is typical of the goriness of this early horror story:

> But he seized her tongue with pincers, as it protested against the outrage, calling ever on the name of her father and struggling to speak, and cut it off with his merciless blade. The mangled root quivers, while the severed tongue lies palpitating, faintly murmuring; and, as the severed tail of a mangled snake is wont to writhe, it twitches to the dark earth convulsively, and with its last dying movement it seeks its mistress's feet.

Philomel manages to convey the gist of what has happened in a tapestry. The two sisters are reunited and take revenge upon Tereus by killing his son Itys and serving his flesh for dinner. But it is only when Philomel bounds into the room, brandishing the boy's head, that Tereus understands the full horror of his meal. He chases the women through the palace, hoping to kill them, but as they run they turn into birds, Philomel into a nightingale and Procne a swallow (Tereus becomes a hoopoe in some versions, the oddest transformation of the three): 'As they fly from him you would drink that the bodies of the two Athenians were poised on wings; they *were* poised on wings! One flies to the woods, the other rises to the roof.'

Sanitized of its bloodthirstiness and overt sexual references, the myth's image of love betrayed, and of a nightingale perpetually lamenting this betrayal, was to be reworked in European song and poetry for the next 1800 years. In twelfth-century France and Spain, it was a popular theme of the troubadours and was repeatedly mixed up with more obvious nightingale associations. In the Provençal language there are some fifty surviving lyrics which contain references to nightingales. The bird represents, at various times, the end of winter and the coming of spring, poetic inspiration, the poet himself, the object of his love, a medium of communication between lovers and, just occasionally, a kind of impish phallic symbol. The famous anthology of vernacular songs and poems written in Latin and known as the *Carmina Burana* (probably compiled about 1230) is full of such versatile birds. Poem 82 ('Fringus hinc est horridum'), for instance, has Philomel apparently exorcizing her memories in the chorus of spring: 'The hill is clothed with flowers, and resounds from the birds; in the woods birds sing together and sweetly chatter; nor does *philomena* cease; she remembers her loss.'

In Poem 179 ('Tempus est iocundum') the poet is being inflamed by the nightingale's florid song, to the extent that he begins to see it as a competitor: 'Silence, *philomena*, for the moment! Rise, song, from my breast! O! O! I am all aflower!' The last lines may be an early attempt at echoing the sound of the nightingale's song.

But Latin can't match the resonant and sensuous tones of Provençal when it comes to celebrating the natural world, and the nightingale poems of French troubadours such as Marcabru and Bernard de Ventadour almost all sound onomatopoeic in performance. Originally, they were probably delivered as spoken monologues over the lightest of instrumental backings, and modern reconstructions in this style, delivered with extravagantly clipped consonants, drawn-out vowels and theatrical pauses, perhaps come closer than any other kind of music to conveying the atmosphere of a nightingale performance:

> Bel m'es quan la rana chanta
> E.l sucs pueja per la rusca,
> Per que.l fiors e.l fueilhs e.l busca
> E.l frugz reviu en la planta,
> E.l rossinnols crid'e brama
> Sa par qu'a per joi conquisa,
> Pies d'orgueilh car el no sen
> Freg ni gel ni glaz ni bisa.

(Marcabru)

(It pleases me when the frog sings and the sap rises in the bark; because the flowers and the leaves and the branches and the fruit return in the plants and the nightingale cries and calls its mate which it has conquered through joy, filled with pride, for it does not feel cold, nor ice, nor winter wind.)

The Philomel myth was largely abandoned by the later troubadours, yet the nightingale could still remind the poet of his losses in love, because of the contrast between the bird's carefree fluency and the poet's mute melancholy:

> I do not sleep neither day nor night, for at night, when I
> go to bed, the nightingale sings and cries, and I, who
> used to sing, die of chagrin and sadness.
>
> (Bernard de Ventadour)

At the close of the troubadour era in the early thirteenth century, the nightingale appears less often as metaphor. There is an increasing sense (as there is in the representation of nature in the visual arts) that the idea of individuality is being respected, that the nightingale is being seen – and heard – as a creature in its own right, a distinct and different species as well as a part of a common Creation. In a decidedly modernist lyric from about 1205, Peire Cardenal suggests that the one thing that is common to poet and nightingale is that they are both misunderstood by the public:

> I sing and I play the flute for myself, for no man except
> me understands my language; the people understand
> what my song says as little as they understand the
> nightingale. And I do not have a tongue that shakes or
> stutters, nor do I know how to speak Flemish or
> Angevin, but the meanness which contains them takes
> away the vision of what is false and what is true.

But outside the strict troubadour tradition, nightingales continued to be a source of ripe imagery. In one of the tales in *The
Decameron*, written by Giovanni Boccaccio between 1349 and
1351, a young girl, Caterina, wants to meet her lover, Ricciardo,
secretly and asks her parents if she may go and listen to the
nightingales sing ('ludir cantar l'usignuolo' – a phrase still in
use as a bawdy euphemism for sex in Italy). Caterina's father is
either extremely dull or not taken in at all by her ruse, as he
later says to his wife, 'See, your daughter is so crazy for the
nightingale that she has taken it and holds it.'

A more subtle variation on the same idea occurs in Marie de
France's twelfth-century verse romance *Laüstic*. The story
itself echoes many of the tropes of nightingale lore and tradition. It has sacrifice, a silenced creature, the bird as a token of
frustrated love. It is full of symbolism, at one extreme being a
darkly Freudian parable, at the other a simple tale of a messenger punished.

A woman from Brittany is married to a respected knight,
but loves another, younger, knight, who lives close by. The two
are unable to meet, but communicate discreetly, talking from
their neighbouring windows and tossing gifts to each other.
They also commune by listening to the nightingale which sings
between their dwellings. But the woman spends so much time
at the window, frequently leaving her bed in the middle of the
night, that her husband becomes angry and asks her repeatedly
why she gets up and where she goes.

'Lord,' she replies, 'anyone who does not hear the song of the nightingale knows none of the joys of this world. This is why I come and stand here. So sweet is the song I hear by night that it brings me great pleasure. I take such delight in it and desire it so much that I can get no sleep at all.'

On hearing this her husband gives a spiteful laugh and has the nightingale trapped. He takes it to her and says, 'Now you can sleep in peace, for it will never awaken you again.' The lady is grief-stricken; and out of spite her husband wrings the bird's neck and throws the corpse at her, 'so that the front of her tunic was bespattered with blood, just on her breast'. Heartbroken, she places the little body in an embroidered shroud and sends it to the knight. They both understand that their distant affair is over. But the young knight is not 'uncourtly or tardy'. He inters the nightingale in a small gold casket and carries it with him at all times, as a memorial to the dreams they shared.

In Britain, medieval nightingale poetry was by and large more jovial and direct. Anglo-Saxon riddles welcomed the bird back as a cheering harbinger of spring. Dafydd ap Gwilym included 'The brooks songstress . . . Beautiful, slim, sweet-spoken' in his 'Mass of the Grove', even though, as a Welshman, he may never have heard the real thing. In *Troilus and Criseyde*, Chaucer has a nightingale serenade Criseyde to sleep in the moonlight, when she dreams of her lover trans-formed into a great white eagle.

The greatest English nightingale work of the Middle Ages is the long and often uproarious allegory entitled *The Owl and the Nightingale*. The poem, written about 1225, probably by an asso-ciate of Nicholas of Guildford, takes the form of a debate between the two birds, representing the two value systems which were beginning to oppose each other in the medieval world: the ascetic, sin-centred philosophy of traditional Christianity and the emerg-ing ideal of free will and individualism. The owl is solemn and sober, the nightingale joyful and light-hearted. The owl believes in the work ethic, the nightingale in the pleasure principle. The owl is an authoritarian, possibly a conservative, the nightingale a liberal with distinct humanist leanings. For 1794 lines the two birds swap quips and insults. They deprecate each other's appear-ance, tastes in food, ways of singing. And despite its underlying seriousness, their debate is carried on with the raciness of a banter between street traders:

> 'Your name is nightingale,' she said,
> 'But chatterbox would do instead,
> Because you're such a gabby pest!
> Let your tongue have a little rest!'

The argument revolves around the birds' respective senses of responsibility and sin. The nightingale sees the owl as full of the miseries of winter and self-restraint, and herself as part of the optimism and joy of spring. ('You sing just like a hen in snow,/And all she sings it is for woe.') The owl, in return, accuses her of encouraging lechery and laziness – and of running off at the first sign of the privations of winter. She reminds the nightingale of what happened the last time she provoked a wife to adultery (a smear that is a distorted reference to Marie de France's *Laüstic*):

> 'And now with low notes, now with high
> You taught her to do shamefully
> And use her body wickedly.
> Her lord found out, before much time,
> And set out traps and spread birdlime
> In hopes he'd catch what caused his shame.
> And click! he had you in his trap,
> And how your shins did feel the snap!'

The nightingale denies that she encourages infidelity. Treachery in relationships is hateful to her, regardless of whether the wife or husband is the guilty party. She would rather encourage true love in a maiden than cruel or heartless relations between married partners.

The argument is not resolved, though the nightingale has marginally the better of it. What the owl disparagingly describes as the nightingale's 'writelinge' – literally 'chirping', but standing one feels for 'chirpiness' in a more general sense – seems by the end of the poem to be a rather good way to approach the travails of life.

From the sixteenth century there was a renaissance of classical verse, and English nightingale poetry began increasingly to revive the myth of Philomel and Procne, and its sister legend of the nightingale singing with its breast against a thorn. Poems from the early part of the sixteenth century cheerfully mix the myths with medieval double entendres about sharp things in the night. John Lyly (*c*.1554–1606) talks of the bird's 'Brave prick-song!':

> What bird so sings, yet so does wail
> O tis the ravished nightingale
> Jug, jug, jug, tereu, she cries,
> And still her woes at midnight rise.

('Jug' was semi-onomatopoeic slang for the sexual act.)

In Barnabe Barnes (*c*.1569–1609) the reference is a shade more explicit: 'I'll sing my Plain Song with the turtle doves/And Prick Song with the nightingales', and becomes quite unambiguous in the anonymous and saucy 'Song' (*c*.1600, see p. 66), and in John Marston's ditty from *The Dutch Courtesan* (1633):

The dark is my delight
   So tis the Nightingales.
My Musick's in the night,
   So is the Nightingales.
My body is but little,
   So is the Nightingales.
I love to sleep against prickle
   So doth the nightingale.

Other poems make a more mawkish identification with the abandoned and stricken bird. 'O Philomela fair, O take some gladness,' bewails Sir Philip Sidney (1554–86), 'That here is juster cause of plaintful sadness:/Thine earth now springs, mine fadeth,/Thy thorn without, my thorn my heart invadeth.' Richard Barnfield (1574–1627) admits that 'For her griefs so lively shown/Make me think upon mine own.' Joseph Warton's ode (*c*.1745) is addressed to 'Contemplation's favourite bird!':

O fail not then, sweet Philomel,
Thy sadly warbled woes co tell;
In sympathetic numbers join
Thy pangs of luckless love with mine!

At various times, Richard Braithwaite, Patrick Hannay, John Milton, William Blake and Matthew Arnold all composed gushing tributes to the grieving bird. Shelley, surprisingly, was scarcely any better. His allegorical poem, 'The Woodman and the Nightingale', closes with the stanza: 'The world is full of

Woodmen who expel /Love's gentle Dryads from the haunts of love, /And vex the nightingales in every dell.' And his 'Semichorus of Spirits from his 'Prometheus Unbound' is as indigestible as anything from two centuries before:

> There the voluptuous nightingales
>   Are awake through all the broad noonday,
> When one with bliss or sadness fails,
>   And through the windless ivy-boughs,
> Sick with sweet love droops dying away
>   On its mate's music-panting bosom.

But there were isolated writers who stood aside from this doleful tradition. Izaac Walton, in *The Compleat Angler* (1653), appropriates the bird as a kind of avian angel, but gives a joyous and precise account of the song.

> . . . the nightingale . . . breathes such sweet loud musick out of her little instrumental throat, that it might make mankind think that Miracles had not ceased. He that at midnight (when every labourer sleeps securely) should hear (as I have every often) the clear airs, the sweet descants, the natural rising and falling, the natural doubling and redoubling of her voice, might well be lifted above earth and say 'Lord, what Musick has thou provided for the Saints in Heaven when though affordest bad men such musick on Earth.'

William Cowper (b. 1731) – who mistook some other bird for a nightingale on New Year's Day (see p. 20) redeemed himself with the delightful 'The Nightingale and the Glow-worm', in which the worm persuades the bird not to eat it, out of a kind of workers' solidarity: ''twas the . . . self-same Power Divine/ Taught you to sing and me to shine.' And the most resilient and probably best-known nightingale lyric of all, the folk song titled variously 'The Soldier and the Lady', 'The Bold Grenadier', or 'The Nightingale', comes straight out of the medieval tradition of ribald euphemism. Cecil Sharp heard half a dozen versions of this on his folk-song collecting expeditions in the Southern Appalachian mountains in North America, where they had been taken by English settlers in the sixteenth century. This version was recorded in Somerset in 1906, but it could be matched by lyrics from Carolina or Kentucky – or Suffolk.

As I was a-walking one morning in May
I saw a fair young couple as they was walking
    this way,
O she was a fair maid, a beauty, I declare
And the other was a soldier, a bold grenadier.

Kind kisses and compliments as they both did
    walk together
Till they both did come down by the side of
    some river,
When they sat down together by the clear
    crystal stream.
Hark, hark, said the fair maid, how the nightingales
    do sing.

When he softly clasped his arms all around
    her middle
And out of his knapsack he pulled out a fiddle.
He played such a tune my boys made the
    valleys ring.
Hark, hark, said the fair maid, how the nightingales
    do sing.

7

'… the merry Nightingale'

from

'The Nightingale. A Conversation Poem'

No cloud, no relique of the sunken day
Distinguishes the West, no long thin slip
Of sullen light, no obscure trembling hues.
Come, we will rest on this old mossy bridge!
You see the glimmer of the stream beneath,
But hear no murmuring: it flows silently,
O'er its soft bed of verdure. All is still,
A balmy night! and though the stars be dim,
Yet let us think upon the vernal showers
That gladden the green earth, and we shall find
A pleasure in the dimness of the stars.
And hark! the Nightingale begins its song,
'Most musical, most melancholy' bird!
A melancholy bird? Oh! idle thought!
In Nature there is nothing melancholy.
But some night-wandering man whose heart was pierced
With the remembrance of a grievous wrong,
Or slow distemper, or neglected love,
(And so, poor wretch! filled all things with himself,
And made all gentle sounds tell back the tale
Of his own sorrow) he, and such as he,
First named these notes a melancholy strain.
And many a poet echoes the conceit;
Poet who hath been building up the rhyme
When he had better far have stretched his limbs
Beside a brook in mossy forest-dell,
By sun or moon-light, to the influxes
Of shapes and sounds and shifting elements
 Surrendering his whole spirit, of his song
And of his fame forgetful! so his fame
Should share in Nature's immortality,
A venerable thing! and so his song

Should make all Nature lovelier, and itself
Be loved like Nature! But 'twill not be so;
And youths and maidens most poetical,
Who lose the deepening twilights of the spring
In ball-rooms and hot theatres, they still
Full of meek sympathy must heave their sighs
O'er Philomela's pity-pleading strains.

My Friend, and thou, our Sister! we have learnt
A different lore: we may not thus profane
Nature's sweet voices, always full of love
And joyance! 'Tis the merry Nightingale
That crowds, and hurries, and precipitates
With fast thick warble his delicious notes,
As he were fearful that an April night
Would be too short for him to utter forth
His love-chant, and disburthen his full soul
Of all its music!

           And I know a grove
Of large extent, hard by a castle huge,
Which the great lord inhabits not; and so
This grove is wild with tangling underwood,
And the trim walks are broken up, and grass,
Thin grass and king-cups grow within the paths.
But never elsewhere in one place I knew
So many nightingales; and far and near,
In wood and thicket, over the wide grove,
They answer and provoke each other's song,
With skirmish and capricious passagings,
And murmurs musical and swift jug jug,
And one low piping sound more sweet than all –
Stirring the air with such a harmony,
That should you close your eyes, you might almost
Forget it was not day!

Samuel Taylor Coleridge, April 1798

Coleridge was the first of the Romantics to decisively reject the maudlin associations of pastoral poetry and return to the optimistic, joyous bird of the medieval period. In his 'conversation poem' 'The Nightingale' he refers to the tradition (quoting Milton's words, 'Most musical, most melancholy bird') only to dismiss it as the conceit of self-pitying poetasters who had never truly listened to the bird: '. . . some night-wandering man whose heart was pierced/ . . . And so, poor wretch! filled all things with himself,/ And made all gentle sounds tell back the tale'. He suggests that the tormented poet might have done better to have gone for a tramp in the woods and surrendered himself 'to the influxes/Of shapes and sounds and shifting elements'.

This is what Coleridge himself had done. It was the spring of 1798 and he was staying with his wife Sara at Nether Stowey in the Quantocks, a couple of miles away from William and Dorothy Wordsworth's house, Alfoxden Park, near Holford. The two men were deep into their momentous collaboration on the *Lyrical Ballads,* and in the company of Dorothy (but not Sara) they often walked at night in the woods round Holford. 'The Nightingale' describes one of these expeditions in late April to a copse near Dodington Hall, just north of the Holford-Stowey road. Coleridge addresses the poem to his companions – 'My Friend, and thou our Sister' – but the 'conversation' implicitly includes the reader too, who is led by the hand into the 'moon-lit bushes': 'Come, we will rest on this old mossy bridge!'

The date of the poem's origin is supported by a letter Coleridge wrote to Wordsworth in early May 1798, enclosing a manuscript draft of the poem. The letter contains a marvellous snatch of doggerel which confirms Coleridge's refusal to take a solemn view of the nightingale:

> In stale blank verse a subject stale
> I send per post my Nightingale;
> And like an honest bard, dear Wordsworth,
> You'll tell me what you think, my Bird's worth.
> My own opinion's briefly this –
> His bill he opens not amiss;
> And when he has sung a stave or so,
> His breast, & some small space below,
> So throbs & swells; that you might swear
> No vulgar music's working there.
> So far, so good; but then, 'od rot him!
> There's something falls off at his bottom . . .'

'The Nightingale' is remarkably accurate in its insights into the bird's habits and natural history. Coleridge knows that it is only the male nightingale that sings, and that serenading males 'provoke' each other. He also understands the bird's habitat (the 'grove is wild with tangling underwood'), but places it, tellingly, in a derelict mansion, 'which the great lord inhabits not', making the vernacular singer displace the absentee aristocrat. And as Coleridge's stanzas echo with the rhythm and rattle of the song itself, so the bird becomes (as it was to become for Keats) a symbol of freedom as well as joy: . . . 'Tis the merry Nightingale/ That crowds, and hurries and precipitates/ With fast, thick warble his delicious notes . . .'.

Twenty years later, on 11 April 1819, Coleridge and Keats met on Hampstead Heath. They walked and talked for not more than three-quarters of an hour, but ranged, according to a letter by Keats, over continents of topics:

In those two Miles he broached a thousand things – let me see if I can give you a list – Nightingales, Poetry – on Poetical Sensation – Metaphysics – Different genera and species of Dreams – Nightmare – a dream accompanied by a sense of touch – single and double touch – A dream related – First and second consciousness – the difference explained between will and Volition – so [many] metaphysicians from a want of smoking the second consciousness – Monsters – the Kraken – Mermaids – Southey believes in them – Southey's belief too much

diluted – A Ghost story – Good morning – I heard his
voice as he came towards me – I heard it as he moved
away – I had heard it all the interval – if it may be
called so.

Though Keats obviously regarded Coleridge's bombastic
monologue as something of a joke, it may well have stirred in
him the first thoughts of the nightingale ode. It had been a
dispiriting time in his personal life. He could see no way
forward in his intense love for Fanny Brawne (who was living
next door at the time the ode was written). One brother,
George, had emigrated to America and the other had died of
tuberculosis. John was only twenty-three but, from his
medical training, had begun to suspect that he too was in the
early stages of TB. His move to the clean air of Hampstead
and the Vale of Health in 1817 had been partly prompted by
this fear. But the spring of 1819 seemed to offer some cheer.
The weather was perfect. Between 26 April and 18 May there
was an almost unbroken run of balmy, dry days. Everything
was in a state of luxuriant forwardness. Roses were in bloom
on 3 May, and nightingales seemed to have returned to north
London early and in some numbers. In Highgate, at least,
their songs were voluminous enough to keep the dyspeptic
Coleridge awake at night. (He punned about his misfortune
in a letter to a friend: 'Ah! PHIlomel! ill do thy strains accord
with those of CALomel!') One bird had already taken up
residence in the shrubberies of Wentworth Place, where Keats

was living, and he confessed to feeling 'a tranquil, continued joy' at its song.

And one fine morning, quite possibly May Day itself, he took his chair from the breakfast table into the small, secluded garden, sat under the plum tree, and wrote 'Ode to a Nightingale' in two or three hours. The Wentworth Place bird may have been singing at the time, but Keats was soon in a reverie and dreaming of more distant, poetic nightingales. He thinks of the bird's other home, and how he, too, may need to migrate to the 'warm South' for a cure; of his brother's terminal illness ('youth grows pale, and spectre-thin, and dies') and how the bird's joyous song is, and has always been, a challenge to death and decay, to 'The weariness, the fever and the fret/Here, where men sit and hear each other groan'. He wonders, not too seriously, if it might be 'rich to die/To cease upon the midnight with no pain/While thou art pouring forth thy soul abroad/In such an extasy!' But he rejects the idea, almost as if it were an insult to the bird to walk out on the beauty and vitality concentrated in its song.

The musing takes him through 'faery lands', the forested landscape of 'white hawthorn and pastoral eglantine' he had encountered in Dryden's version of the medieval nightingale poem, 'The Flower and the Leaf'. And meditating on all the generations of listeners who have been touched by the bird, he catches, just for a moment, a vision of the oneness of the world. The nightingale's song transcends him, unites singer and listener, human and nature.

But then the reverie breaks. Even if the song is immortal, the nightingale itself is not, and, a real, mobile bird again, it flies away over the heath. Keats himself is 'tolled' back to his 'sole self' – but not, I think, to such an anti-climactic state as some critics of this stanza would argue. To have caught the tension – and the resonance – between the immortal nightingale of the imagination and the flesh-and-blood bird is one of the poem's great achievements.

It was an idea for which he was in debt to William Hazlitt. In the spring of 1818, Keats had attended Hazlitt's course of lectures on the English poets. The fifth lecture, on Thomson and Cowper, made a particular impression on him. In this, Hazlitt extends the argument that he first laid out in his famous essay 'On the Love of the Country' (1814). What distinguishes our fondness for nature from our other attachments, he suggests, is its 'abstractedness': 'The interest we feel in human nature is exclusive, and confined to the individual, the interest we feel in external nature is common, and transferable from one object to all others of the same class.' As Hazlitt extends his argument, so the inspiration for many of the images, feelings and even phrases in Keats' ode become clear:

> If we have once enjoyed the cool shade of a tree and
> then been lulled into a deep repose by the sound of a
> brook running at its foot, we are sure that wherever we
> can find a shady stream, we can enjoy the same pleasure
> again, so that when we imagine these objects, we can

easily form a mystic personification of the friendly power that inhabits them, Dryad or Naiad, offering its cool fountain or its tempting shade.

Hazlitt's lecture ends with the example of familiar birds, with the nightingale itself, and with the prototype of one of the most powerful phrases in Keats's poem. 'The cuckoo,' he writes, '"that wandering voice", that comes and goes with spring, mocks our ears with one note from youth to age; and the lapwing, screaming round the traveller's path, repeats for ever the same sad story of Tereus and Philomel!'

8

'Provençal song, and sunburnt mirth'

Proud Songsters

The thrushes sing as the sun is going
    And the finches whistle in ones and pairs,
And as it gets dark loud nightingales
    In bushes
Pipe, as they can when April wears
    As if all Time were theirs.

These are brand-new birds of twelve-months growing,
    Which a year ago, or less than twain,
No finches were, nor nightingales,
    Nor thrushes
But only particles of grain,
    And earth, and air, and rain.

Thomas Hardy, from *Winter Words,* 1928

Nightingales' songs can seem approachable, prosaic even, as well as mesmerizingly romantic. Certainly, there are times when they make me ponder the same themes as Keats – lost youth, mortality, the continuity of nature, the hedonism of the south. But more often they seem to me to be singing in the spirit of Coleridge's 'merry' bird and the impish punster in 'The Owl and the Nightingale'. I have found their 'writelinge' seductive, skittish, ebullient, heartening, often comic, but almost never melancholy, and over the years they have come to seem like familiars, albeit of a rather distant and elusive breed.

I often daydream about them in the winter months, working them into fantasies of escape to the sun. I imagine them as accompaniments to Provençal picnics, as cooling as fruit in the afternoon heat. And to moonlit suppers in white-stoned Andalucian villages (and then, on a more absurd flight of fancy, I try to imagine the best wine for drinking with the song). I think, too, of the times they have lured me out on more homely expeditions – of mild, clear nights in bluebell time in England and the sudden urge to point the car towards Suffolk. It is always a dream of heading off, of migration. I become like Rat in *The Wind in the Willows*, fretting at the onset of autumn and beguiled by the Sea Rat's tales of the Mediterranean and the swallows' 'intoxicating babble . . . of violet seas, tawny sand and lizard-haunted walls'.

Only twice did I hear nightingales on my home patch in the Chilterns. In the 1980s, one settled in the woods at Ashridge, and I took my ageing mum on a rare trip out to hear it. A few years later one sang all spring at a run-down municipal rubbish-tip about a quarter of a mile from my house. Its home was a steep thicket, wedged between the main Euston railway line and a battery of waste incinerators. The A41 to London was less than two hundred yards away in the other direction, and much of the time the bird was scarcely audible above the roar of trains and traffic. I first heard it at midnight one evening in mid-May, singing against an orange full moon and the glow of rubbish fires started by fly-tippers, and was lost in admiration at its magnanimity. But I fretted that it might be a solitary and unstimulated bird. There were certainly no other singing nightingales within earshot, and probably not within ten miles. I am not even sure it had a mate. Some nights I would lean out of my window and wonder if, with a lull in the traffic and a change in the wind, I might hear a snatch of the song floating into my bedroom. But I suppose that was a dream of escape, too.

In Suffolk, some years before, I had listened to them from my bedroom window. I owned a cottage in the Blyth valley for a while, and they sang the very first night I moved in. It was another hot mid-May and I had driven up to Suffolk with the car windows wound right down. All the way through the tracts of heathland that stretch from Aldeburgh to Walberswick, nightingale phrases flew, disembodied, into the car.

That night two sang close to my cottage, one in the churchyard, another in the scrubby heathland that began just fifty yards beyond the garden. I lay awake all night listening to them, puzzling about why I found their songs so poignant and evocative. A few days later at Minsmere bird reserve on the coast, I heard an extraordinary duet between a nightingale and a nightjar. It was about an hour after sunset. The nightjar lay silhouetted along the branch of a dead oak, looking like a woody extrusion itself and turning its head slightly as it poured out its dry, reeling song. Six feet below it a nightingale sang from the deep wrappings of a blackthorn bush, in the kind of bravura performance that must have helped give rise to the old myth about the breast against the thorn. They sang together, drone and counter tenor, for nearly fifteen minutes. I had met up with a group of birders from Teesside and we stood in a silent row, marvelling at this apparition of the southlands only eighty miles from London. Then we all went and drank to them at the Eels Foot pub, which lies on the margin between the heath and the marsh.

※※※※※

I was going to write that nightingales take me out of myself, transport me. But it is often just the opposite. They make connections. They have been reassurances about fortuitous beauty and the continuity of nature and place, a kind of mascot or charm. Often I have heard them unexpectedly, on workaday business in what I thought were familiar landscapes: along a bushy green lane in Selborne, when I was trying to trace the extent of Gilbert White's own territory; sounding from a remote wood in the New Forest, when I thought I was lost; chanting against the roar of Phantom jets flying out of Lakenheath air base in the sandy wastes of the Suffolk Breckland. And on each occasion I have understood in a new way where I was.

Once I was so decisively put back in place by them that they helped me overcome an odd and intractable phobia about being 'abroad'. I'd done a bit of exploring in southern Europe in my early twenties. I travelled down through Spain, swapping guitar licks with flamenco players and watching bee-eaters hawking from the telegraph wires. I spent a summer in Provence, and one dawn crept out over the Camargue salt-pans to watch the flamingo flocks close to. Then work and the responsibility of helping to nurse my invalid mother, stopped me venturing overseas. I soon got so out of the habit that the prospect began to fill me with dread. It wasn't a fear of flying or exotic illnesses, but of what John Clare described as 'being out of one's knowledge'. I would have nightmares of waking in a foreign house and not knowing where I was, of being unable to get home again, of having no control over what was happening to me. When I finally shook off my phobia on a winter weekend in Holland with two staunchly tolerant friends, I took with me – just in case

– a handwritten card to prop up by my bed, saying DON'T PANIC – YOU ARE IN AMSTERDAM. I put the seal on my *rites de passage* later that year with a trip to the French Pyrenees with an old rambling companion. It had been a long and claustrophobic winter in Britain, and we'd mapped out a few days on the Cerdagne plateau, some 3,000 feet up in reputedly the sunniest skies in France. We had fanciful hopes of drifting amongst fields of wild narcissi and drinking Catalan wine under the circling eagles. I imagined there would be nightingales too, but didn't give this familiar bird much thought beside the glamorous creatures of south-western France. I was after something new to confirm my rediscovered adventurousness.

Our drive down from Toulouse started well. There were dazzling clear skies, and packs of returning swifts flickering through the mountain passes (bound for England, we hoped!). We ignored the way patches of snow seemed to be edging ever closer to the sides of the road, and had got as far south as Ax-les-Thermes before we realized that we were driving slap back into winter. All the way through the snaking curves of the Col de Puymorens the snow was banked in high drifts by the sides of the road. There were no flowers, and the little greenery that was visible had been bent double by fresh snowfalls during the past few days. Our Pyrenean suntrap was frozen in, and after a brief conference we aborted our plans, cancelled the hotel, and headed off south-east, towards the Mediterranean.

It seemed a disastrous decision at first. We were going down-hill now and the hairpins were vertiginous and exhausting. We had the wrong maps, the wrong clothes, and no clear idea of where we were heading. The temperature rose steadily, and I became increasingly disorientated by the landscape. By the time we had reached the coastal plateau, I was remembering all too fearfully the phantoms and anxieties that had trapped me in England for so long. Then the ancient clarion came to my rescue. We were passing a long cypress windbreak on the outskirts of Perpignan when, out of one of the trees, a nightingale flung a fierce, explosive phrase. In a moment, but in a way I can't properly explain, I had my bearings again. It was May, we were in the South of France, and all creatures (ourselves included) were in their proper place.

Perpignan, an effervescent Catalan town with streets smelling of dried herbs and warm laundry, proved to be a marvellous base. We spent most of our time in the maquis, the Mediterranean scrub belt of pistacia and evergreen oak, with its elaborate and motley understorey of aromatic and spiny shrubs – cistus, rosemary, lavender, box, juniper. The maquis was full of nightingales. And they seemed to be singing wherever we went, in scrub-filled roadside ditches, in overgrown farmyards, in scraggy copses of stone pine and kermes oak – anywhere there was a patch of bushy cover. They sang throughout the daylight hours in brief, intense snatches, and more flamboyantly in the evenings. But they never became mundane, just a persistent bubbling undertone to almost everything we did, like the sound of running water.

Sometimes they were more vehement. One clammy afternoon we did a tour of the little villages in the Tech valley listening to the local bands and spending too much time inside the car. On the way back to Perpignan we stopped to stretch our legs in an abandoned quarry. It was a bizarre landscape. There were the relics of tiny, opportunist vineyards and overgrown hedges. Thin wisps of smoke curled through the heat haze. There was a nightingale in almost every patch of scrub, and by the time we reached the centre of the quarry, we could hear at least a dozen singing at once. We also realized that the smoke was not blowing from some spontaneous fire in the parched scrub, but from a pile of smouldering mattresses. We were in the local rubbish-tip.

But a half-memory of places like this from twenty years back (or something glimpsed unconsciously out of the corner of an eye) was nagging me, and I felt that we must go and look at a sheer quarry face about 300 yards away. I did not even need to raise my binoculars to know what the spectre was when it finally broke cover and shot vertically upwards. It was a bee-eater, as florid as an aerial exhibitionist as the nightingale is as a singer. We ran forwards and were able to get within about a hundred yards of what proved to be a group of six, lounging against each other on a tree at the top of the quarry face. And as the nightingales contin-ued their chorus, the bee-eaters whizzed about, sometimes darting upwards after prey, sometimes gliding down then sud-denly changing direction, so that their chestnut backs shone in the sun one moment and their turquoise underparts the next.

On our last day I heard my first hoopoe. We were meandering about, listening to nightingales and admiring a meadow full of lax-flowered orchids, when I heard a sound that I thought at first had come from some kind of farm animal. To tell the truth it sounded rather like a gibbon. Then it came again, a triple-horn note, and I guessed it must be a hoopoe, a bird I had never heard call before. A few seconds later I saw it fly up into a dead tree, like an immense butterfly striped in ginger and black. I raced after it – followed smartly by the farmer up whose back drive I was now jogging. He enquired – in raspy *langue d'oc*, but very courteously – whether I had any problems. I dug to the depths of my fossil French and tried to explain a chase I would have had difficulty justifying in English. But communication more ancient than national tongues came to my rescue. The hoopoe's name is onomatopoeic, and, after I had pooped a few times, the farmer's eyes cleared and he said, '*Ah, l'huppe. Son nid est dans le chêne.*' In an instant, vestigial agoraphobia and a week's fuming at *chasse gardée* signs evaporated, and I relished the supreme satisfaction of making contact *abroad*.

An almost ruined holiday had been well and truly rescued. So, I reckoned, had I, venturing out as a timid greenhorn and returning with a new confidence as a traveller. The nightingales and their exotic companions had a lot to do with the transformation. They seemed for those few days a kind of bridge – effervescent citizens of the south, but also reliable, comprehensible fellow creatures.

I have heard nightingales in many parts of southern Europe since. One sang in a solitary myrtle bush in front of a Costa Brava beach development. Another year, they staked out their pitches like buskers in the small north Majorcan village where I was staying with friends in April. One lived in the lemon grove behind the house; he serenaded us as we sipped drinks on the balcony at sunset and watched the black vultures circling to roost above the crags. Another sang much later in the night, from the depths of a garden that we toiled past on our way back from the restaurant.

My favourites haunted the tangled edges of the River Dourbie in the limestone country west of the Cévennes. During the 1990s this became my favourite patch of France, an almost annual destination, and its nightingales acquired a rather laid-back urbanity, like young cronies from the local bars. One late-May night, under a full moon and a sky lacy with stars, three riverside birds with territories about a hundred yards apart sang at midnight, in strict order, for just five minutes each. In this place of highly local character (Auden called the southern limestone 'this region of short distances and definite places'), singing in one's own spot at one's own special moment is enough to establish identity.

The one thing nightingales never became for me were the Cupids beloved of medieval troubadours and modern songwriters. But for the time Lily and I were together, nightingales – and for that matter many other kinds of bird – insisted on being part of the relationship. She lived in a cottage in Surrey, the nightingale's one-time heartland, the site of Tennyson's and Gerard Manley Hopkins's poems and Beatrice Harrison's celebrated cello duet. Lily had heard one in her garden the year before we met, and in spring there were always chiffchaffs and blackcaps singing yards from her window. (She also kept geese, which she insisted on calling 'gooses'. It was a piece of affectionate whimsy that still makes my throat catch and which so touched me with its note of respect that I have tried to remember since that nightingales, too, are individuals, and not members of that abstract collective '*the* nightingale').

With that heightened perception that sometimes accompanies romantic affairs, I soon rediscovered a slight gift for intuiting and predicting where we might see unusual birds. I succeeded in conjuring up a great grey shrike on Frensham Common and a short-eared owl on same north Norfolk marsh I had seen one twenty years before. Wherever we went we saw woodpeckers, usually in pairs, and they became a tongue-in-cheek private symbol for us, and a way of imagining what the other was doing or thinking when we were apart. ('One was carrying a stick,' Lily said hopefully after a pair flew past early one spring.)

She was playing a sophisticated vamp in a TV comedy series at the time, and when she was interviewed by a listings magazine about her own most romantic dream, she replied 'listening to nightingales with someone you are fond of, and not having to talk'. I don't believe that either she or the magazine knew of the anciently ribald meaning of the phrase. But I did, and liked to think it was beamed specifically at me.

Anyway, the idea of genuinely listening to nightingales together turned from a whim into a serious yearning; and failing totally to find any in Surrey that year, we planned a trip to the South of France, starting in Lily's favourite Dordogne and moving down to the Languedoc. I didn't know what to expect from the Dordogne, which is so often mocked for having become a kind of pastoral theme park for the English. But it reminded me of a southerly version of the chalk downs. The Dordogne river itself is hundreds of yards wide during its passage through the limestone, and is edged by shallows and bays and wild willow thickets. On our first evening we sat side by side on the bank in a haze of sound. Fish were jumping, crickets scratching and behind us, from a poplar grove, came the liquid, musing warbles of golden orioles. We heard our first nightingales together as we were walking back to the hotel. They were bustling about in riverside scrub by a wooden bridge, and active enough to be visible. I was far too excited to have the gumption not to talk.

Thereafter the perfectly romantic nightingale, communed over in silence, eluded us. Roadside birds sang in such extravagant ensembles that they demanded not just talk but programme notes. Hotel birds were usually too distant. In Domme there were several singing outside our bedroom window, but first Lily was detained in the bathroom as a consequence of a surfeit of *eau de noix,* then I lost my hearing aid. By the time we were both composed the birds had stopped singing.

It didn't really matter. By the river, or in the hilltop villages on the ridge, bird song and sun seemed to melt preset resolutions and soften boundaries. Whenever we sat outside a cafe, there was always a black redstart darting about from window-ledge to rooftop above us, its terse, metallic song ringing down the street. Near the River Lot, we heard a wryneck chiming *inside* a hollow walnut tree. And just as there had been when I was in southern France years before, there were nightingales everywhere, whatever the conditions. We even heard them singing or at least whistling brief, consoling phrases to themselves – 3,000 feet up in the cool, mist-wreathed heights of the Corbières hills, in scrub thick with sodden orchids.

By the time we reached the edge of the Mediterranean zone the weather had begun to turn. We decided to put up for one night in an auberge in the spa village of Alet les-Bains, on the banks of the River Aude. It was a gloomy hotel in what seemed to me a soporific town, and as the atmosphere turned more humid and oppressive, I had, to Lily's understandable bemusement, a return of my old twinges of disorientation and anxiety. Nowhere seems more entrapping than a small town under a flat grey sky. But the hotel, set at the edge of a derelict medieval abbey, had its own healing powers. That evening, we sat outside, drank black wine (Ricardelle de la Clape!) and filled ourselves with cassoulet. The cloud passed, the hotel garden filled up with garrulous tourists and Alet-les-Bains began to seem a very agreeable place. At dusk the owls started, the heavy boom of eagle owls in the distance and a cacophony of tawnies in trees all around the hotel. We stole out through the garden, and by the walls of the ruined abbey saw them flickering through the hotel lamp light, followed by a stream of bats. At our feet the glow worms were coming alight, and we felt enchanted.

Our room, too, seemed a relic of the Middle Ages, with a bed as bowed as a glaciated valley and a sit-up tub for a bath. We laughed ourselves to sleep, while outside the nightingales did their best to serenade us against the roar of the river.

9

'Hidden as a thought unborn'

from
The Nightingale's Nest

Up this green woodland ride lets softly rove
& list the nightingale – she dwelleth here
Hush let the wood gate softly clap – for fear
The noise might drive her from her home of love
For here Ive heard her many a merry year
At morn & eve nay all the live long day
As though she lived on song – this very spot
Just where the old mans beard all wildly trails
Rude arbours oer the rode & stops the way
& where that child its blue bell flowers hath got
Laughing & creeping through the mossy rails
There have I hunted like a very boy
Creeping on hands & knees through matted thorns
To find her nest & see her feed her young
& vainly did I many hours employ
All seemed as hidden as a thought unborn
& where these crimping fern leaves ramp among
The hazels underboughs – Ive nestled down
& watched her while she sung – & her renown
Hath made me marvel that so famed a bird
Should have no better dress then russet brown
Her wings would tremble in her extacy
& feathers stand on end as 'twere with joy
& mouth wide open to release her heart
Of its out sobbing songs – the happiest part
Of summers fame she shared . . .

Sing on sweet bird may no worse hap befall
Thy visions then the fear that now decieves
We will not plunder music of its dower
Nor turn this spot of happiness to thrall
For melody seems hid in every flower
That blossoms near thy home – these harebells all
Seems bowing with the beautiful in song
& gaping cuckoo with its spotted leaves
Seems blushing of the singing it has heard
How curious is the nest no other bird
Uses such loose materials or weaves
Their dwellings in such spots – dead oaken leaves
Are placed without & velvet moss within
& little scraps of grass – & scant & spare
Of what seems scarce materials down & hair
For from mans haunts she seemeth naught to win
Yet nature is the builder & contrives
Homes for her childrens comfort even here
Where solitudes deciples spend their lives
Unseen save when a wanderer passes near
That loves such pleasant places – Deep adown
The nest is made an hermits mossy cell
Snug lies her curious eggs in number five
Of deadened green or rather olive brown
& the old prickly thorn bush guards them well
& here we'll leave them still unknown to wrong
As the old woodlands legacy of song

John Clare, *c.*1832,
from *The Midsummer Cushion*,
first published 1978

Both the public history and the personal experience of nightingales seems inexorably qualified with associations and metaphors. Yet sometimes this compulsive desire to find meanings in the song can seem like taking liberties with the bird. The nightingale is a creature in its own right, not just a symbol or a source of happenstance background music. Even Gilbert White, a deeply sympathetic lover of birds, distanced himself from presumptuous claims about – and to – the bird's song. In 1789, just ten years before the publication of the *Lyrical Ballads* (which marked the formal beginning of the Romantic movement, and included Coleridge's 'conversation poem' on the nightingale), he wrote that 'the language of birds is very ancient, and, like other ancient modes of speech, very elliptical: little is said, but much is meant and understood.' But White meant understood by other birds, not by us. Whatever is going on when we listen in to nightingales, it certainly isn't a dialogue between us and the birds.

The poet Kim Taplin came up against this conundrum – the recognition that she was being touched by a voice that made no rational sense to her – one summer in Oxfordshire. She was walking along the River Cherwell close to her home, amongst the bankside tangle of alder and nettle and meadowsweet. It was a humid afternoon, and, hot and stung, she retreated to the shade. And 'obliged to give up trying to possess the secrets of the place and sit quietly, they had a chance to take possession of me'.

Then she heard – without any intention or preconceptions – a bird singing from the undergrowth. It wasn't a nightingale and probably not the local rarity, a marsh warbler. In fact she was not sure what kind of bird it was. That was what struck her so powerfully about the song. It was not full of specific warbler codes or elaborate symbols, but seemed to be pared down to that most fundamental of natural signals: 'fellow creature here':

> Its song . . . was full of delight but it did not have me
> rapt, nor was it wistful or cheerful or any of the
> anthropomorphic adjectives we use in trying to 'capture'
> birds' song in words. And I have no view on whether it
> sang 'I love you' or 'Keep off' to some invisible mate or
> rival. I only knew that it seemed to sing itself, as it was
> itself, without self-consciousness, and that I felt
> immeasurably lucky to be there.

She instinctively felt, too, that it seemed to live there by a more certain right than her own.

I understand her feelings. Yet I have never been able to feel entirely excluded from a nightingale's performance, or from its habitat. When I listen to a bird, any bird, singing, I don't feel like an intruder or voyeur (as I do sometimes when, say, watching feeding or mating). I know that, strictly speaking, I am, that the singing is neither for my benefit nor the benefit of most other birds, but is scored for and directed at neighbours of the same species. But it still seems too public, too indiscriminately thrown into the air, too capable of arousing human emotions to be neatly compartmented off like that. Rightly or wrongly, I feel *included*.

And one early June afternoon in Provence, surprised for once to be in the audience, I realized I was truly *listening* to a bird for perhaps the first time, not probing it for symbolism or poetic resonance, but just trying to hear what it was doing. It was very hot, and we'd taken a break from driving for a stroll through the fields. I hadn't expected a nightingale (it was late in their singing season) but one started up, hesitantly, in a thicket by the lane. We sat down in the shade of the bushes and just listened. It wasn't a loud singer and certainly not a virtuoso. Its phrases were short, modest and had a kind of reflective, inward quality, with plenty of staccato clips but none of the classic flaring crescendos. But the bird persisted and the performance began to build into something pleasingly structured and compact. I began to wonder what determined the order of the phrases. The idea that the bird was consciously choosing each one, as if it were writing a score, strained even my bird-biased credulity. But so did the notion that it was firing them off automatically, much as a computer on a random selection programme might do. This model, apart from denying the bird any agency, doesn't fit well with the fact that most nightingales' songs become more complex over the spring, as they 'practise' more and hear and recollect other birds' phrases.

Across the lane the rows of lavender bushes were just beginning to show purple. I could hear the shouts of children playing in the village stream. And the phrase 'absent-minded' drifted into my head – which of course doesn't at all mean the mind is absent but describes a state where concentration drifts in and out of full conscious awareness. As if to prove my point, the nightingale, unusually, repeated a quiet but elaborate phrase twice, as if it was suddenly pleased with what it had just expressed. Chit-cherwit-chevy-pelew is how I recollect it.

We can never know what is going on in the consciousness of a bird when it is singing. But that languorous afternoon I felt I could begin to understand the nightingale if I regarded its singing as an analogous to my own 'absent-minded' whistling when I'm preoccupied, something which is partly unconscious but also dependant on my stored musical knowledge and mood. Maybe the closest musical analogy would be improvised jazz, where each new phrase isn't so much consciously worked out as flowing spontaneously and organically from the one before.

When I first went on the trail of nightingales, I was struck by how often they seemed to choose some kind of natural amphitheatre to perform from. In my first spring in Suffolk – that hot May full of nightingales – I heard birds in all kinds of arenas. Perched one early morning on the edge of a sunken tennis court on Aldeburgh common (approximately where the umpire might sit), I listened while a bird served short, piercing phrases from dense scrub behind the baseline, filling the glade of shorn grass and straight white lines with an incongruous wild skirling. A few miles to the north I came across the remains of a Second World War gun-emplacement, half swallowed up by steep barrows of blackthorn, broom and gorse. Its concrete base was already too hot to sit on in the late morning sun, but that diminutive hollow, smelling of peach and coconut from the broom flowers, was the focus of another nightingale's fitful but tireless noon-time song.

What is going on here? Do the birds have a taste for spaces which add sonorousness to their song? Is there anything in the old belief that they favour sites where there is an echo? Or is it simply a matter of my choosing a miniature arena to listen in, of seeking a hideaway in the bushes in much the same way as the bird itself? I have made burrows like this, places to lie up, ever since I was a child, and maybe this has helped make me instinctively sympathetic towards the bird.

The secretiveness of nightingales can make them seem like outlaw birds, creatures of the maquis, singing against the world. It is an association which has been emphasized by their reputation for singing during trench fighting and bombing raids – cocking a snook at the war, or playing the heroic bugler, depending on who is relating the story. They probably do not sing more than other species in these conditions (many birds are provoked by loud noise), but they are remarked on more, for the poignant irony of exquisite song co-existing with the chaos of battle – which is of course a dramatic irony, of which the audience is aware, but not the players.

I heard nightingales once on the Ministry of Defence's tank-training ranges at Tyneham in Dorset, just a few days after the Chernobyl nuclear reactor had blown up in 1986. It had been the worst of all possible springs. At the beginning of May, three days after the explosion, the hedgerows were still silent and shrivelled, and the sky the colour of church-roof lead. Then a pressure front loaded with radioactive isotopes had sent numbing winds across most of Europe. It did not seem to deter the nightingales. Tramping the ranges during the second weekend in May, I heard their songs floating up against the gales. They were singing, it seemed, from *under* the ground, from old shell craters that now brimmed with dense blackthorn scrub. In the charged atmosphere of that day their songs seemed wildly ambivalent – pathetic, indomitable, indifferent; swan-songs of defiance. But they, of course, knew nothing of this and were, as Kim Taplin wrote, just singing for themselves.

Yet in some situations they have been used almost thera-peutically. For generations there has been an annual bluebell-and-nightingale picnic at Tiger Hull, a wood close by

Arger Fen in Suffolk. The adjoining house was owned by the Christian Socialist doctor Grace Griffiths, and the picnic is held every April in her memory. The paterfamilias of Suffolk writers, Ronald Blythe, was a regular guest, and he recalled how 'Clear as the chiffchaff somewhere above our heads, Dr Grace's familiar voice re-enters our consciousness, patient, learned, faintly cracked, as she told us how to identify birds and flowers.' She had run the house as a sanatorium for tuberculosis patients, who were wheeled out into the hillside wood even in the depths of winter. 'We saw them lying on beds in the snow, waving when we waved, thin arms with big hands, brave grins and sometimes even a shout' They were wheeled out in the spring, too, to listen to the nightingales – 'whole choirs of them singing together in those days' – recalling Keats' view of them as an antidote to 'the weariness, the fever and the fret' of the luckless consumptive.

<hr />

It was the Northamptonshire poet John Clare who most closely located the common ground between ourselves and the bird in his poem 'The Nightingale's Nest'. It is a work which sums up his lifelong hostility to the over-weening appropriation of nature. In the winter of 1824 he had written to his publishers Taylor and Hessey stating unequivocally what he thought about current urban attitudes to nightingales:

I forgot to say in my last that the Nightingale sung as common by day as night & as often tho its a fact that it is not generally known your Londoners are very fond of talking about this bird & I believe fancy every bird they hear after sunset a Nightingale I remember when I was there last while walking with a friend in the fields of Shacklewell we saw a gentleman & lady listening very attentive by the side of a shrubbery and when we came up we heard them lavishing praises on the beautiful song of the nightingale which happened to be a thrush but it did for them & they listend & repeated their praise with heart felt satisfaction while the bird seemed to know the grand distinction that its song had gaind for it & strive exultingly to keep up the deception by attempting a varied & more louder song the dews was ready to fall but the lady was heedless of the wet grass ... such is the ignorance of nature in large Citys that are nothing less than over grown prisons that shut out the world & all its beautys.

Clare may well have numbered his publishers among such gushing amateurs. But he quite probably had Keats in mind, too. In a letter written nine years after Keats's death, he criticizes the poet for describing 'nature as she ... appeared in his fancys & not as he would have described her if he had witnessed the thing he describes'. To Clare the essence of poetry was faithfulness to both the observed, material world and to the imagination, the 'poetic eye'. He was, as the critic Hugh Haughton has pointed out, above all the poet of *seeing*.

Clare knew nightingales as fellow creatures of the copse long before he knew their status as poetic symbols and as what he called 'the popular voice of music'. When he was a boy he loved to listen to their 'restless song' as he passed their 'black thorn bower', and knew them from several sites in his home village of Helpston, on the edge of the Cambridgeshire fens. Every year nightingales nested in Royce Wood, close to the village, and Clare's journals and notes are full of observations about the bird. He describes its skulking habits whilst feeding in the undergrowth and its great reluctance to fly in the open. He mentions that he has never once found a nest without oak leaves. He notes a thrush which learned phrases from a nightingale, and gives a vivid account of the quiet song sometimes heard in the proximity of the nest: 'she whistled without effort – never raising the feathers of her throat & neck & head as I had seen her but piping as quietly as the Robin & as if the song came almost involuntary without her knowing it'

And after this observation (made in May 1832, when he was living at Northborough, three miles from Helpston), he confesses that he is wrong to have called nightingales 'she' and that he is '*almost* certain that the female is silent & never sings'. In the same year he makes the best attempt that exists in nineteenth-century literature to transcribe the notes of the song, from a bird singing in the orchard outside his window:

Chee chew chee chew chee
chew – cheer cheer cheer
chew chew chew chee
– up cheer up cheer up
tweet tweet tweet jug jug jug

wew wew wew – chur chur
woo it woo it tweet tweet
tweet jug jug jug

tee rew tee rew tee rew – gur
gur – chew rit chew rit – chur-chur-chur
chur will-will will-will tweet-em
tweet em jug jug jug jug
grig grig grig chew chew

wevy wit wevy wit
wevy wit – cheet-chit
chee-chit chee chit
weewit weewit wee
wit cheer cheer
cheer – pelew
pelew pelew –
bring a jug bring a
jug bring a jug

Clare makes no attempt to suggest any mood or affective meaning behind the different phrases. Instead of trying to 'understand' the song, he sings it himself. And readers who also sing or say it, out loud, will find they pass through a portal between two sound worlds. Clare has transcribed a song for human voices, but its insistent precision somehow conjures up a bird's experience. It brings to my mind the striking phrase used in another context by Sean Street in his study of bird song, *Wild Track* – 'the poetry of information'.

All Clare's experience of the bird and its habitat – which is also *his* habitat – is worked into 'The Nightingale's Nest'. The poem begins in much the same way as Coleridge's tribute. The reader is taken by the hand and led into the poem by the device of being led into the thicket (Royce Wood) itself: 'Up this green woodland ride lets softly rove/ & list the nightingale . . .' Yet though Clare shares Coleridge's view of the song – 'its luscious strain . . . the happiest part/Of summers fame she shared' – he does not listen to it at a distance, as a member of an audience. Clare knows this wood as well as the bird does; he shares its territory: '& where these crimping fern leaves ramp among/ The hazels underboughs – Ive nestled down/ & watched her while she sung. . .' Unlike Keats's nightingale, which is fabulous, immortal, abstract, Clare's is a particular bird, placed in an exact spot inside the territory of the parish ('Aye as I live her secret nest is here/Up on this white thorn stulp'). Clare isn't glibly identifying with the bird, but he does see it as a fellow commoner, making a livelihood on the marginal lands, even wearing similar garb: '. . . her renown/ Hath made me marvel that so famed a bird/ Should have no better dress than russet brown.'

It is also a fellow artist, a maker not just of music but of an exquisite, unpretentious nest – 'an hermits mossy cell' – whose construction he spells out in affectionate detail. But Clare goes to some length to differentiate himself from the bird, and would, I think, have agreed with John Berger's words: 'Art does not imitate nature, it imitates a creation.' He is meticulous in celebrating the nightingale as an individual, something exterior to himself. He understands its fears and, respecting its privacy, finally leaves it 'still unknown to wrong/As the old woodlands legacy of song'. The song is both his and the bird's. The old woodland is both Royce Wood and all of England's ancient forest, a once common heritage which he had witnessed being whittled away by enclosure and appropriation in his own lifetime. If 'The Nightingale's Nest' celebrates the individuality of both poet and bird, it also warns about their shared vulnerability.

The old woodland's legacy has continued to be looted. The landscape on the edge of the Cambridgeshire fens which Clare said 'made my being', has been enclosed, drained, uprooted, ploughed and added to the indistinguishable arable wastes that now stretch from Lincolnshire to central Suffolk. When I last walked through it was hard to believe that I was in the same country Clare wrote about. Royce (now Rice) Wood has become a manicured forestry plantation. The hollow lanes have been straightened or stopped up. His 'pleasant places' – Langley Bush and Puddocks Nook and Hilly Snow, his blackthorn clumps and pulpit oaks – have been levelled and obliterated. I was there in mid-May, nightingale time, but in most of Clare's old spots there was not even the possibility of a nightingale.

Only on the remains of Emmonsales (or Ailsworth Heath, now Castor Hanglands National Nature Reserve) have the birds clung on. This is three miles south of Helpston and was at the very edge of Clare's confined and frugal world. He had strayed there when he was very young and had 'rambled among the furze the whole day till I got out of my knowledge when the very wild flowers and birds seemd to forget me and I imagined they were the inhabitants of new countrys . . .'

On that mid-May morning, with grim aptness, the heath hung under a dank mist. At noon my breath was still coming out in wintry clouds, and the cowslips and cuckoo flowers underfoot were bent under the weight of dew. I heard the first nightingale about 200 yards away, its song muffled by the fog to a ratchety staccato. It was warming up more than singing, firing off short, disjointed phrases and clipped end-notes, like semi-colons. Another joined in about thirty yards away, in blackthorn scrub which had been heavily browsed by sheep and deer. I heard just one more that day, at the other end of the reserve, which seemed a sad total for what had once been the best local site for the bird. I recorded it on an old cassette machine, and played it down the phone to Lily.

Later I learned that nightingales had been declining on the reserve since a high point in the early 1980s. Wherever I went that summer the story was the same. At Kingley Vale, the great horseshoe of yew wood and chalk scrub that opens out on to Chichester harbour, there was not a single bird. In the late 1960s this had the highest density of birds ever formally recorded in England (13.8 pairs per square kilometre). Since then, the warden, Richard Williamson, told me they have dwindled away, two pairs only between 1985 and 1990 and then none at all.

The decline round Selborne had followed almost the same pattern. Since 1962 Stephen Povey had regularly cycled along the lanes that join Oakhanger and Worldham, just north of the village. They are lined with deep, some times double, hedges and tracts of old coppice woodland. On a May evening in 1962 he counted twenty-three singing nightingales along the three-mile route. By 1974 the number had dropped to eleven (I heard four in a single stretch of this road in 1981), and by 1985 to three. Since 1987 there have been no birds along this route, nor anywhere else in the entire parish. Throughout England the nightingale has now retreated south-eastwards and is only present in any numbers in Suffolk, Essex and Kent. Yet even the extreme south-east can no longer offer anything like the experience of the Kent survey in 1970. In a long vigil between midnight and dawn on 24 May 1967, observers heard – and with remarkable composure, logged – 977 separate nightingales. The UK population has plummeted from tens of thousands of pairs in the 1950s to little more than 5,000 today. Between 1995 and 2020 alone, surveys by the British Trust for Ornithology suggest an alarming decline of nearly 50 per cent. The causes of this crash (which is evident all over Europe) are complex. They almost certainly include climate change, which has aggravated droughts in Africa and caused exceptional spring storms and frosts on the birds' northward migration routes through the Mediterranean. But the dramatic halving of insect populations across Europe over the same period, as a result of intensive chemical farming, is most probably the chief cause, as it is of the decline of many insectivorous bird species.

The consequence in Britain has been to make the nightingale even more a creature of rumour and mythology, and less the real-life bird-of-a feather celebrated by John Clare.

10

'Magic abroad in the air'

from

A Nightingale Sang in Berkeley Square

That certain night, the night we met,
there was magic abroad in the air.
There were angels dining at the Ritz,
And a nightingale sang in Berkeley Square.

The moon that lingered over London Town,
poor puzzled moon, he wore a frown,
How could he know we two were so in love,
The whole darn' world seemed upside down,

The streets of Town were paved with stars,
it was such a romantic affair,
And as we kiss'd and said 'goodnight'
A nightingale sang in Berkeley Square.

When dawn came stealing up, all gold and blue,
to interrupt our rendezvous,
I still remember how you smiled and said,
'Was that a dream, or was it true?'

Eric Maschwitz and Manning Sherwin, 1940

Even between the wars, the nightingale must have seemed like a bird from mythology for most people in Britain – not so much because its slow decline may already have started, but because the human population now largely lived where nightingales did not, or could not, live. Although they can be accommodating village birds in England, they have never haunted urban areas in the way they sometimes do in mainland Europe (e.g. Berlin).

It was to try and bring the song to city dwellers that Beatrice Harrison hatched her famous plan to broadcast the bird's song live from her garden in Surrey. She was by a long margin the most distinguished British cellist in the 1920s. Delius dedicated his Cello Sonata to her. She was Elgar's favourite soloist and he chose her to make the first recording of his Cello Concerto. In 1922, when she was thirty, she moved with her family to Foyle Riding, an isolated house set in woodland south of Oxted in Surrey. The following spring the weather was fine enough to tempt her into practising in the garden, sitting on a rustic seat set in a sea of bluebells. One afternoon she was in the middle of Rimsky-Korsakov's 'Chant Hindou' when a bird began to sing along with her. She was understandably astonished and began to trill up and down the scales. The bird, she reported, followed her notes 'in thirds, and always perfectly in tune with the cello'. The gardener identified the bird as a nightingale and congratulated Beatrice on bringing it back to Foyle Riding, after years of absence.

Early in 1924 she made her broadcasting debut, in a performance of Elgar's Cello Concerto (conducted by the composer) at the Central Hall, Westminster. Halfway through, touched by the thought of the many thousands of listeners she was playing to, she hatched the idea of broadcasting the nightingales that sang in her wood. She was determined to present the plan to Lord Reith, Director General of the fledgling BBC, himself, but had a long tussle persuading him to support it. Reith argued, in terms that are still familiar, that the cost would be prohibitive, the birds unpredictable, and that he would be accused of killing conversation and encouraging second-hand experiences. What would happen, he protested, if people preferred listening to the nightingale singing from the loudspeaker rather than from the woods and lanes? (He referred to the 'tinned nightingale', perhaps recalling Hans Christian Andersen's story.) Beatrice, for her part, pleaded the cause of all those who had no access to woods and lanes in their daily lives, let alone real nightingales, arguing that the song could not fail to uplift them.

Her trump card was the fact that the birds would now burst into song whenever she played her cello in the woods. Lord Reith, elitist and puritan though he was, was also a broadcaster and realized that he could create something of a coup – the very first live outdoor broadcast – at the same time as salving his conscience. Art coaxing nature into a euphonious duet was altogether different from a piece of ornithological vox pop. Reith gave the scheme his personal support. There was a trial, which went well, and the broadcast was scheduled for the evening of Saturday 9 May.

Two van-loads of equipment and a large battalion of engineers arrived at Foyle Riding that day and set up the operation in the garden. The microphone was placed as close as possible to the bird's usual singing post, and the amplifiers were stacked in the summerhouse. The broadcast had been announced in advance, with much trumpeting in the press, and the plan was to wait until the bird was in full song and then break into the Savoy Orpheans' Saturday night dance programme.

Beatrice put on her best concert frock and went out into the garden to play for what was likely to be the biggest audience of her life. It was a clear, warm night with a full moon. So that the microphone could pick up both the bird and her cello, she had been positioned in a ditch close to the bush in which the bird usually performed. 'I placed my chair half in and half out of it, quite crooked, but I knew the exquisite voice was there, under a thicket of oak leaves, ready .to sing to his little wife.' But he proved to be a very shy serenader. Beatrice tried playing 'Danny

Boy', parts of the Elgar concerto and snatches of Dvořák, all to no avail. Donkeys brayed, engineers tripped over in the dark, rabbits gnawed the vital cable, but no nightingale sang.

Then, just after 10.45, twenty minutes before the station was due to go off the air, the bird began. An excited continuity announcer broke into the Orpheans, and for the next fifteen minutes the BBC's audience listened entranced to the historic duet. And 'duet' isn't a fanciful description of the performance. Although the BBC wasn't able to record that first live broadcast, repeats in succeeding years show that, though the bird doesn't literally follow or copy the music, it is clearly responding to the phrases coming from Beatrice's cello, like a loosely improvised cadenza over a bass ground.

At least that was the story at the time. In recent years something like a conspiracy theory has grown that the broadcast was a fake. The voice broadcast that night belonged not to a bird, but to a professional bird mimic or siffleur, Maude Gould, known as Madame Souberon on the variety circuit. The corporation had signed her up as an insurance policy, in case the nightingale proved erratic or was frightened off by the crew and their recording equipment. So at the point when it became clear the bird wasn't going to oblige, Madame Souberon was given her cue. Recent searches in the BBC and Harrison family archives have found no evidence whatsoever that this happened. Instead eye-witness accounts from those present confirm that the recording was authentic, and the real bird did sing on time.

And the broadcast was a sensation. A million people listened in, many of them hearing a nightingale's song for the first time. It was picked up as far afield as Italy, Paris, Barcelona and Hungary – and in regions like Scandinavia and Scotland where nightingales had never been heard. Many listened on crystal sets, and those who didn't have their own receivers enlisted friends to relay the broadcast to them over the telephone. In some places where the radio (or its loudspeaker) was out of doors, listeners reported the broadcast spurring other nightingales into song. Over the months that followed Beatrice Harrison received 50,000 letters of appreciation. It was almost as if the act of broadcasting, putting the nightingale one stage further removed from the listeners, had heightened its already secretive appeal.

Beatrice Harrison proved to be a great champion of the birds. On a tour of America with a programme of performances and talks, she regularly gave out her home address to audiences, inviting them to visit Foyle Riding and hear nightingales for themselves – an invitation which many hundreds took up. On 13 May 1933 she held a Nightingale Festival at the house, to raise money and support for the Royal Society for the Protection of Birds, and especially for Lord Buckmaster's bill to outlaw the catching and selling of skylarks. Foyle Riding was open from 4 p.m. till dawn the following morning. The magazine *Bird Notes and News* ran a report on the day: 'The nightingales happily did not disappoint listeners, for when they sank into silence and possibly disapproved of the lights of a mile of motor cars that flowed over the car parks, the chinks of plates and many voices, Miss Harrison wandered down with her magic instrument and lured them to song again.'

The 'Cello and Nightingale' experiment was repeated with great success in June that year, and then made an annual event – and always on these subsequent broadcasts, with the songs of real birds. On one occasion, when it was staged in a damp part of the wood, the cello set off a chorus of frogs, which was faithfully broadcast as part of the ensemble performance. It continued for twelve years, until Beatrice Harrison moved house, and was then carried on sporadically, featuring the unaccompanied birds, until 1942. The nineteenth of May that year should have been, to the day, the eighteenth anniversary of the first broadcast. What happened instead became a historic recording in the BBC archives. The operation got under way as usual, with tantalizing uncertainty. The birds were fitful, the broadcasters on edge. But after two or three false starts, Sam Bonner, duty engineer for the evening, felt they were singing well enough for him to authorize the break into the late-night dance-music programme. Then, through his headphones, he became aware of the distant hum of approaching aircraft. It was, we know now, the beginning of the 'Thousand Bomber' raid on Mannheim. Bonner knew nothing of the details, but realized that this was not the kind of noise to broadcast live during the middle of a war. He made an urgent call to his London producer, Franklin Englemann, to shut down the broadcast transmission. Fortunately he was also aware that what was happening was a unique piece of actuality, and asked for access to a recording channel. One was quickly made available and, as a result, there still exists a long and unsettling record of this duet between a single nightingale and a fleet of bombers, as extraordinary in its own way as the performances with the cello. The throb of the aircraft swells remorselessly for nearly four minutes before ebbing slowly away for another three, and for the whole duration of the record the nightingale sings unwaveringly. Over that painfully stretched time its song becomes an indomitable warning note against which you cannot escape meditating upon the different faces of war. The bird persists, indifferent to human folly. Beauty co-exists with horror.

By contrast Eric Maschwitz and Manning Sherwin's song 'A Nightingale Sang in Berkeley Square' is unashamedly escapist. Yet it too is about the paradox of song in the midst of strife. It was written in 1940, at the height of the Blitz, and is as much an evocative picture of London at war as a story of enraptured lovers. The city is under black-out, bathed in moonlight as it has not been for centuries, so that its streets are 'paved with stars'. A nightingale seems to sing from the silhouetted trees in the square, and the starstruck lovers forget the stresses of war and imagine the bird singing just for them: 'I still remember how you smiled and said, "Was that a dream, or was it true?"' – echoing Keats' reverie, two centuries earlier : 'Was it a vision, or a waking dream/ Fled is that music – Do I wake or sleep?'

Just as nightingales occasionally imitate human music, so, for centuries, music-makers and composers have tried to capture or copy the bird's song. There is even a small whistle-like instrument called the nightingale which was used to mimic the bird by Scarlatti in his Oratorio, and by Haydn and Romberg in their 'Toy' symphonies. The lower part of the whistle is held in a glass of water, so that when blown it produces a clear, bubbling tone, a little like some of the bird's simpler phrases. In Hans Christian Andersen's story 'The Nightingale', the Chinese court ladies, smitten by the 'lovable coquetterie' of the song, achieved the same effect by putting water in their mouths, 'so as to gurgle when anyone spoke to them'. Schubert, Gounod, Saint-Saëns, Tchaikovsky, Rimsky-Korsakov and Handel all wrote pieces inspired by or echoing the song. Respighi actually incorporated part of an early phonograph recording of the bird's song into performances of his orchestral piece *Pines of Rome*.

The most lyrically evocative – though of a very reflective and languorous bird – is probably Granados's 'Quejas, o la inaja y el ruisefior' (Lament, or Beauty and the Nightingale) from his piano suite *Goyescas* (1911); and the most naturalistic, the duet between the woodlark and nightingale in Olivier Messiaen's *Catalogue d'Oiseaux* (1956–8). Messiaen was fascinated by bird songs from an early age, and was gifted with an ear acute enough for him to transcribe them in the wild. The songs, of course, couldn't be accurately reproduced inside the restrictions of conventional notation: birds sing in freer rhythms and at pitches which only occasionally correspond to

Western chromatic scales. But what Messiaen was able to write down was sufficiently 'true' to act as a catalyst for his own compositions. (Like John Clare he saw analogies between the acts of singing and composition.) In the *Catalogue d'Oiseaux* he combines these reworkings of the rhythm and essential structure of the song with an atmospheric, tonal picture of the natural habitat in which the performance is taking place. These are his own evocative notes of the woodlark/nightingale duet:

> From the col of the Grand Bois at St-Sauveur en Rue, in the mountains of the Forez. Pinewoods to the right of the road, meadows to the left. High in the sky, in the darkness, the Woodlark peel off two-by-two: a chromatic, fluid descent. Hidden in a thicket, in a clearing in the wood, a Nightingale responds, its biting tremolos set in contrast with the mysterious voice on high. A Woodlark, invisible, draws near, fades. The trees and fields are dark and still. It is midnight.

But Messiaen can't avoid being anthropocentric. His work is framed by the precepts and limitations of human music and Western scales. What might music be like if it considered nightingales' own auditory universe? Birds' sense of hearing is more acute and discriminating than ours, and their songs compress musical information at pitches and speeds which are beyond the scope of human ears. (Some single nightingale notes, for instance, are only 1/150 of a second long.) The only way these details can be brought into our perception is to slow the songs down to a quarter or even an eighth of their 'natural' speed.

The composer David Hindley experimented with this technique in the late twentieth and early twenty-first centuries, extending it to meticulous computer-assisted analysis and musical notation of the songs. He anatomized the songs of the woodlark and skylark (200 notes a second in some trills) and reconstructed them inside musical compositions. He also transcribed the nightingale's song from recordings (he never heard a 'live' one), and then transposed it. At quarter speed the song is barely recognizable. It becomes an eerie recital of modernist effects – slides, whoops, percussive trills. Most remarkably, what seem like single notes at natural speed resolve at slow speeds into sonorous, velvet chords of up to four discrete notes (birds' syrinxes are able to produce more than one note simultaneously). It is like the orchestrated noise of a whole tropical forest and, to human ears, has little of the pleasant, accessible musicality of the song at normal speed. Yet for Hindley it echoed the expressionism of early-twentieth-century music, with the regular appearance, for instance, of sliding notes and fourths and fifths, the 'perfect intervals'. He also found familiar musical devices, many of them opposites of one kind or another, regularly and directly juxtaposed: loud and soft, high and low, short and long, single note and chord.

Birds even seem to 'enjoy' their songs, in the same way as humans. The songs of juvenile birds, for instance, aren't utilitarian territorial advertisements, but are soft, free-flowing, playful. This 'immature', improvisatory style (to which adults sometimes revert) may have a rough structure which is innate and unique to each species, but this does not mean that it is entirely automatic. It is spontaneous and inventive and seems to have much in common with the play of young mammals. Even when birds are singing territorially in the breeding season, their songs are far from crudely functional. The distinguished ornithologist Charles Hartshorne wrote in 1958:

There is without doubt a good deal of utility. But it is not the narrowly bound immediate utility of growl, whine or alarm-note; its results are not usually to be brought about the next moment, but only in the course of hours or days (a long time for a bird); they are not limited to a single outcome, but to several very different ones (securing a mate, warning rivals off territory, maintaining the pair bond). Since there is not an immediate and single practical meaning for song, it will not have a crude or narrowly emotional character, like sheer hostility as in growls, or sheer misery as in some piteous howlings, but will be such as to fit a more balanced and normally cheerful, though mildly excited state, such as is suitable both to interest in a mate and to interest in the privacy of territory. Be it noted that maintaining a territory – and still more, attracting a mate – is only intermittently a desperate, all-or-none affair like keeping possession of a meat-bone. It is, much of the time, leisurely and pleasant; there is seldom an extreme emergency, when anything terrible can happen quickly. It is not to be imagined that a bird engaged in territorial singing for hours is exclusively reacting to the possibility of a successful invasion. There is ample room, and some probable need, for its activity to be sustained by the interest of the activity itself, both as a muscular exercise and as the production of a pattern of sound which the bird itself is well aware of.

The idea of bird song as an expressionist – or at least expressive – form may help explain why we respond to it. Even hard-line behaviourists now broadly agree that song is a fundamentally a vehicle for expressing the bird's 'emotional tone', its intricate demonstration of a willingness to hold territory, its response to the weather, the strength of its bond with its mate and even its satisfaction with its own vocal performance. Complexity, loudness and duration, for instance, may be positive qualities for a male songbird, but they have the imprint of human registers of machismo.

Recently scientific ornithologists have put forward what they call 'the Smart Cookie' theory about nightingale's song: female nightingales interpret 'good' songs (loud, long, complex) as indicators of health and an ability to protect territory and feed young. This is a hugely anthropomorphic assumption, and its fallacious analogue in the human world – glamorous voice indicates reliable husband – ought have been a warning to the scientists. When the female bird chooses her mate more subtle qualities, evident only to her and members of the same species may be just as aphrodisiac. Singing abilities are doubtless partly genetic, and a more plausible theory might be that the female bird chooses simply for singing ability alone, something which will be passed down as a desirable quality through the generations . . . Yet all these reductionist, competitive theories fail to explain how birds with what scientists regard as poorer singing skills succeed in finding mates.

The evolutionary biologist Richard Dawkins makes an alternative suggestion in *Unweaving the Rainbow*. Taking his cue from the phrase in Keats' 'Ode' – '. . . and a drowsy numbness/Pains my sense as though of hemlock I had drunk' – he argues that the idea of a nightingale song acting like a narcotic is not far-fetched. Some ornithologists may think of the song as conveying precise information about the male bird's breeding condition. But, Dawkins suggests, 'another way to look at this has always seemed to me more vivid. The song is not informing the female but *manipulating* her. It is not so much changing what the female knows as directly changing the physiological state of her brain. It is acting like a drug.' And, to round off the analogy, it isn't that surprising that it also manipulated the mind of John Keats and, by extension, any human listener. Birds and human are both vertebrates, and drugs which work on humans have similar effects on other vertebrates. Dawkins concludes with clinical logic: 'Natural selection has had thousands of generations in which to fine-tune its drug technology.'

The kind of neurological process that Dawkins describes is known to happen when humans listen to their own music. There are so many suggestive and reciprocal links here that it might be as appropriate to call music 'bird-song-like' as to describe bird song as musical. The American naturalist David Raines Wallace has suggested that our brains may retain, at the deepest level, the structures and mental charts of our reptilian and bird-like ancestors: 'I suppose this is why so many people feel a sense of affinity with birds. Our admiration for their bright colours, sweet songs, and graceful flight suggests that some very large part of our brains is still up in the canopy with them . . .'

Certainly the most basic human music, like bird song, shows playfulness, utility and direct expression of feelings. A good deal of folk-song even shares the precise musical characteristics of nightingale song – gapped scales, common occurrence of perfect intervals, improvisation within a set structure, frequent pauses. Cecil Sharp, on his Appalachian folk-song collecting expeditions, also noted echoes of a kind of territoriality in vernacular music, with particular songs associated with particular places and times in the daily life of the community. One singer, unable to recall a song, said, 'If only I were driving the cart home I could sing it at once.'

I'm not sure what I feel about these reductionist, evolutionary theories. Dawkins' especially seems suspect, rooted as it is an increasingly questionable male-focused biology. But so too are our attempts to press the song into the human-shaped moulds of 'poetry' or 'music'. I have to say that, for me, the experience of listening to nightingales has never felt like a close encounter with my cultural ancestors. I can see the evolutionary and structural steps that might lead from bird song to music, but my feelings refuse to follow them. I have no instinct for appropriating or subsuming or even identifying with the bird. The nightingale I hear on a May night is not a prototype, a roughcast early link in some great cultural Chain of Being that leads inexorably upwards to Bach or Keats, but a complete and finished creature, different from me in ways that I cannot even imagine, yet still able to move me. Its 'otherness' is what touches me, more even than the common ecological threads between us. By 'singing itself' in such a pure and irreducible way it seems to challenge and chasten any listeners singing less than themselves.

Listening to nightingales with a new respect over recent years, I've found those 'self-same songs' oddly reassuring. They provided consolation during the break up of a relationship and a thread of continuity that helped keep us friends afterwards. (I was pleased to discover that nightingales have 'friendly' sub-songs, too – relaxed, platonic carollings in the sub-tropical woods in winter.) They have kept loneliness and anxiety at bay in strange places. But I've also heard the ominous silence of sites that nightingales have abandoned, and know that the myths and metaphorical power cannot survive without the real bird.

This is the theme of what must be the most sympathetic and respectful of all nightingale stories. The bird in Hans Christian Andersen's tale lives in the woods surrounding the lavish palace of a Chinese emperor. He is summoned to court to sing, and enchants not just the Emperor but the whole population. But one day a parcel arrives for the Emperor containing an artificial nightingale, ornamented with jewels and driven by clockwork. The court, ever capricious, is charmed, and the mechanical bird is set up for a duet with the real nightingale. It is a disastrous experiment. The mechanical bird keeps strict tempo and jars terribly with the free-flowing style of the real bird, which promptly flies back to the woods.

For a while the artificial nightingale is all the rage. It sings the same predictable, precisely measured song every time. The citizens learn to whistle its tune. The palace band performs concerts with it. Then, five years later, the Emperor falls fatally sick. The mechanical bird is worn out and past helping him. But at the last moment the real nightingale begins to sing outside the Emperor's window, and pulls him back to life. (Death flies out of the window, struck by 'a yearning for his garden'.) The Emperor implores the nightingale to stay with him, but the bird offers instead another kind of relationship:

I can't make any home at the palace, but do you let
me come here when I like. Then I will sit at evening
time on the branch there by this window and sing to
you, to make you happy, and thoughtful too. I will
sing about the happy and about those who suffer. I
will sing of the evil and the good that is about you
and is hidden from you.

Softened though it is for a children's story, this is the same
nightingale – wild, free-spirited, truly romantic – that sang for
Keats and Coleridge, that held listeners spellbound in front of
crackly 1920s radios, that I have heard myself under the full
moon, and that John Clare crouched close to, listening to an
elegy for the old woodlands that were being flattened around
him. It is the nightingale in which the real and metaphorical
birds merge, one way of celebrating what it feels like to be alive
in this place at this moment.

ᘈᘈᘈᘈᘈ

It's the May full moon again, and I'm back in east Suffolk. But it's
a different kind of evening, charged with the edginess of our
changing planet. It's 11 pm, and the car thermometer is register-
ing just 2°C. There is the faintest sparkle of frost on the heather.
I've been roaming the heathland around Westleton and
Dunwich, which supposedly houses one of the densest populations of nightingales in England, and haven't heard a single

bird. Is this climate change coming home to roost, exorcizing the spirit of the warm south? The nightingale is vanishing across its traditional range, its population halved over recent decades, and no one is entirely sure why. There's been little nightingale habitat lost in this period, compared to the ravages of the 1960s and 1970s. There have been subtle changes in the density of bushy cover, though that seems hardly sufficient to explain this huge loss. The most likely reason is more chilling, that the birds are declining because their food source – the great legion of summer insects – is crashing from the combined impact of chemical farming and unseasonal weather.

It's midnight now. These are dismal facts to be pondering on a May evening, and raise the spectre that the nightingale may become just a bird of mythology for all of us. I stop at the end of the lane for one last try – and, quite abruptly, one starts up. It's in a dense clump of rhododendrons in a cottage garden, a setting as incongruous as as the temperature. It flings out a few icicle-sharp notes and then stops. But it's a decisive statement: 'I'm still here, *despite* . . .' George Meredith's intense, loquacious poem, 'Night of Frost in May', describes just such an encounter, when on a 'plumed and armoured night . . . There chimed a bubbled underbrew/With witch-wild spray of vocal dew'. The poem argues that the clash of the seasons, and the confusion of feelings this produced, clarified the meaning of the song. Meredith hears 'the lyre of earth . . . it holds me linked;/Across the years to dead-ebb shores/ I stand on, my blood thrill restores.'

Our communion with nightingales remains mysterious. Maybe we intuitively recognize the power and inclusivity of *voice*, when expressed by a non-human with such clarity. Maybe we too feel the pulse of rising spring sap. 'The lyre of earth' says it all for me.

Notes and References

6   Alfred Tennyson, 'Aylmers Field'

10   Percy Bysshe Shelley, Semichorus from 'Prometheus Unbound', 1820

18   Matthew Arnold, 'Philomela'

19   Garth Christian, 'Listening to Nightingales', from *Down the Long Wind*, 1961

30   Stanley Cramp (ed.), *The Birds of the Western Palearctic*, vol. 5, Oxford, 1988

31   Edward A. Armstrong, *A Study of Bird Song*, New York, 1973

33   Margaret Grainger (ed.), *The Natural History Prose Writings of John Clare*, Oxford, 1983

35   H.E. Bates, *Through the Woods*, 1936. Reproduced with permission of Curtis Brown Group Ltd, London on behalf of The Estate of H.E. Bates. Copyright © H.E. Bates.

40   Pliny, *Natural History*, Book X

40–41 Olina, *Uccelliera*, 1662

44   Richard Jefferies, 'Nightingales', first published in the *St James Gazette*, April 1886. See also: W.B. Yarrell, *A History of British Birds*, 1872–4

44–45 'Nightingales who change their tune', *New Scientist*, 14 March 1992

45–46 Francis Willughby, *The Ornithology*, 1628

50   Peggy Munsterberg (ed.), *Bird Poetry*, 1980

52   Sally Festing, *Gertrude Jekyll*, London and New York, 1991

57   Edward A. Armstrong, 'The Evolution of Man's
        Appreciation of Birdsong', in R.A. Hinde (ed.), *Bird
        Vocalisations*, Cambridge, 1969

62–63   P. Stuttard and K. Williamson, 'Habitat requirements of the
        nightingale', *Bird Study*, 18, 1971; Kevin Bayne and Andrew
        Henderson, 'Nightingales and coppice woodland', *RSPB
        Conservation Review*, 1988; R.J. Fuller, 'Distribution of
        breeding songbirds in Bradfield Woods, Suffolk, in relation
        to vegetation and coppice management', *Bird Study*, 39, 1992

66   quoted in Geoffrey Keynes and Peter Davidson (eds), *A
        Watch of Nightingales*, The Stourton Press, 1981

67   A thirteenth-century biography of St Thibaut grouped
        nightingales with other kinds of perniciously seductive
        voices, and obviously felt their metaphorical meaning was
        well enough known to need no further explanation: 'We
        must abandon the field of the Sirens and those of the
        nightingale, who makes many insane, and in all ways we
        must become stronger so that we may near the kingdom of
        Jesus Christ.'

68–71   Wendy Pfeffer, *The Change of Philomel: The nightingale in
        medieval literature*, New York; 1985. See also: Beryl
        Rowlands, *Birds with Human Souls*, University of
        Tennessee Press, 1978

71–73   *The Lais of Marie de France*, translated and edited by Glyn
        S. Burgess, 1986

73–74   J.P. Clancy (ed.), *Medieval Welsh Lyrics*, 1965. Affection
        for the bird wasn't universal in Britain, however. Mary
        Woodward's poem 'Nightingales' relates the story of a

medieval hermit buried in St Albans Abbey who routed the
nightingales from his wood 'because their song disturbed his
prayer': 'Imagine the silent trees, the man alone there making
his continuous lonely devotion to nothing./And the brown
birds' throats warm with joy and music gone for ever.'

74–75   *The Owl and the Nightingale*, Brian Stone (trans.), 1971

80   Cecil Sharp, *English Folk Song from the Southern
        Appalachians*, 1966

87–91   Richard Holmes, *Coleridge: Early Visions*, 1989; H.W.
        Garrod, *Keats*, 1926; Robert Gittings, *John Keats*, 1968;
        Robert Gittings, *John Keats: The living year*, 1954

91   Keats wrote a little panegyric to his sister on 1 May
        containing images similar to those in the ode: 'Please
        heaven, a little claret-wine cool out of a cellar a mile deep .
        . . a strawberry bed to say your prayers to Flora in.'

91–92   Janet Spens, 'A study of Keats's "Ode to a Nightingale"',
        Review of English Studies, vol. 3, 1952

98   Kenneth Grahame, *The Wind in the Willows*, 1908

105   W.H. Auden, 'In Praise of Limestone'

112–113 John Clare, 'The Nightingale's Nest', first published in
        Anne Tibble (ed.), *The Midsummer Cushion*, 1978

115–117 Gilbert White, *The Natural History of Selborne*, 1789;
        Kim Taplin, 'Possession', in Richard Mabey (ed.), *Second
        Nature*, 1984

123–126 Margaret Grainger (ed.), *op. cit.*

123   Hugh Haughton, 'Progress and Rhyme: "The
        Nightingale's Nest" and Romantic Poetry', in Hugh
        Haughton, Adam Phillips and Geoffrey Summerfield
        (eds), *John Clare in Context*, 1994

126   John Berger, 'The White Bird', from *The White Bird*, 1985

128   Steven Povey, 'The Birds of Selborne', *The Selborne Association Newsletter*, 32, 1991; M.E.S. Rooney, 'A report on the status of bird species at Castor Hanglands National Nature Reserve, 1957–1985', Internal Nature Conservancy Council report

128–129 J.T.R. Sharrock, *The Atlas of Breeding Birds in Britain and Ireland*, British Trust for Ornithology, 1976

133   R. Chislett, *Yorkshire Birds*, 1952.

133–138 Beatrice Harrison, *The Cello and the Nightingale*, Patricia Cleveland-Peck (ed.), 1985

141   Messiaen's notes translated by the pianist Peter Hill

142   David Hindley, 'The music of Birdsong', *The Wildlife Sound Journal*, vol. 6, no. 4, Autumn 1990; Joan Hall-Craggs, 'The aesthetic content of bird song', in R.A. Hinde (ed.), *Bird Vocalisations*, Cambridge, 1969; Edward A. Armstrong, 1973, *op. cit.*

143–144 Charles Hartshorne, 'The relation of bird song to music', *Ibis*, 100, 1958

146   David Raines Wallace, *Bulow Hammock*, Sierra Club, San Francisco, 1988. See also: Lewis Thomas, 'The music of *this* sphere', in *The Lives of a Cell*, New York, 1974 Cecil Sharp, 1966, *op. cit.*

147   See Kit Wright's poem 'The sub-song', in *Short Afternoons*, 1989

148–149 Hans Christian Andersen, 'The Nightingale', M.R. James (trans.), London and New York, 1972

Acknowledgements

My thanks to friends who have listened to nightingales with me, especially Roy Adams, Francesca Greenoak, Rachel Hamilton, Robin Hamilton, John Kilpatrick, Anne Mallinson and Peter Newmark.

To Nicola Bion and Alan Cudmore for locating (and lending) elusive books; the staff of the Bodleian library; Roger Deakin; Benny Green, for illuminating some of the history of 'A Nightingale Sang in Berkeley Square'; Sally Haines and her staff at the BBC's Sound Archives; Hugh Haughton, for allowing me to see the unpublished manuscript of his paper on Clare's 'The Nightingale's Nest'; Chris Mead, Robert Fuller and Philip Jackson at the British Trust for Ornithology; Bill Mitchell, whose advice was so helpful at a tangled point in the text; Jane Stemp, librarian at Lady Margaret Hall, Oxford; Richard Williamson; Kit Wright, for his poem 'The sub-song'.

To Penny Hoare at Sinclair-Stevenson for her patience and editorial advice.

And to the friends with whom I had such exhilarating and illuminating discussions about nightingales: Ronnie Blythe for his continued encouragement and his insights into Keats's Ode; Jeff Cloves, who urged me (successfully I hope) to reveal more of my own feelings, and who read the finished text with an inspired eye; David Cobham, who took a wise and objective view of the text; David Hindley, for sharing the revelations of his musical analysis of bird song; Philip Oswald, for thoughts and material on the classical view of nightingales that would have made a whole book in themselves; and Richard Simon, who, as always, was throughout the course of the book a source of support and common sense.

Index